W9-BDD-108

HIGH-INTENSITY TRAINING

the Mike Mentzer Way

Mike Mentzer with John Little

Contemporary Books

Chicago   New York   San Francisco   Lisbon   London   Madrid   Mexico City
Milan   New Delhi   San Juan   Seoul   Singapore   Sydney   Toronto

The McGraw·Hill Companies

Library of Congress Cataloging-in-Publication Data

Mentzer, Mike.
    High-intensity training the Mike Mentzer way / Mike Mentzer with John Little.
            p.   cm.
        ISBN 0-07-138330-1
        1. Bodybuilding.   2. Mentzer, Mike.   I. Little, John R., 1960–
    II. Title.
    GV546.5 .M455   2003
    646.75—dc21   2002067218

3 4 5 6 7 8 9 0   QPD/QPD   1 0 9 8 7 6 5 4 3

ISBN 0-07-138330-1

Cover photograph copyright © John Balik

McGraw-Hill books are available at special quantity discounts to use as premiums and
sales promotions, or for use in corporate training programs. For more information, please
write to the Director of Special Sales, Professional Publishing, McGraw-Hill, Two Penn
Plaza, New York, NY 10121-2298. Or contact your local bookstore.

Permission to reprint interior photographs has been granted by the following copyright holders:

Copyright © John Balik: 12 (right), 43 (right), 49, 52, 63 (bottom), 81 (left), 82, 92 (left), 94, 98, 99, 102, 120 (left and right), 121 (left
and right), 122, 123 (right), 126, 128 (right), 129, 131 (top and bottom), 133, 140 (left), 141, 143 (left), 145 (top and bottom), 146,
148 (left), 150 (left), 153, 161, 163, 166, 171, 181, 182, 188, 189, 190, 192, 194 (left), 196, 208, 211 (left), 212, 213, 214

Copyright © Robert and Gail Gardner: vii, ix, 5, 8, 32, 34, 37, 53, 117, 124, 128 (left), 138, 162, 176, 177, 178, 179, 180, 184, 194
(right), 197, 210

Copyright © Mike Mentzer Estate: 12 (left), 43 (left), 61, 127, 204, 207 (left and right)

Copyright © Michael Neveux: vi, xiv, 18, 20, 28, 33, 57, 58, 59, 64, 69, 72, 73, 76, 86, 91 (left and right), 92 (right), 95, 97, 104, 105
(left and right), 106 (right), 109 (all), 111, 147 (top and bottom), 148 (top right and bottom right), 150 (top right), 155 (left and right),
156, 158, 159 (top right and bottom right), 164, 169, 172, 174, 183, 186, 198

Copyright © Michael Neveux and John Balik: xii, 2, 3, 6, 10, 11, 14, 15 (bottom), 16 (top and bottom), 17, 19, 22, 23, 24, 25, 27, 30,
35, 38, 40, 41, 42, 44, 46, 47, 50, 54, 55, 60, 63 (top), 65, 66, 70, 75, 78 (left and right), 79 (top and bottom), 80, 81 (right), 84, 87,
88, 89, 93 (all), 96, 100, 101, 106 (left), 108 (top and bottom), 112, 114, 115, 116, 118, 119 (top and bottom), 123 (left), 125 (left
and right), 130 (left and right), 132 (left and right), 140 (top right and bottom right), 142 (all), 143 (right), 144 (left and right), 149 (top
and bottom), 150 (bottom right), 151 (left and right), 152, 154, 159 (left), 168, 170, 175 (left and right), 191, 200, 201 (left and right),
202, 203, 205, 206, 211 (right)

Copyright © Northern River Productions: page 15 (top), p. 139

This book is printed on acid-free paper.

To the "new intellectuals": those who are willing to think for themselves and to stand by their decisions; those who believe in principles and act on them; those who seek truth and are willing to share it; those who choose to learn and to educate and who do so in a manner that is both benevolent and ethical. It is to their hands that the torch of Mike Mentzer's legacy is passed, and to them that this book is dedicated.

—J.L.

CONTENTS

PREFACE
MIKE MENTZER (1951–2001)

Within 36 hours of signing the agreement for this book, Mike Mentzer died in his sleep of a heart attack. There had been a congenital predisposition to heart troubles in the Mentzer family. Mike's father, Harry Mentzer, had also died prematurely from cardiac problems, and in what would seem like something out of a Greek tragedy, Mike's younger brother, Ray, would die from the same cause a mere two days after Mike's passing.

Both his life and his death speak to the issue of genetics that Mike had stressed so often and so resolutely in his writings and seminars, for genes, as he often said, are the prime determinant of not only muscular success, but overall health and longevity. Mike received the genes to achieve muscular (and I dare say philosophical) greatness, but he was shortchanged, genetically speaking, in the department of overall health and longevity. We were lucky to have him as long as we did, and I believe that were it not for his training wisdom, which he so diligently applied throughout his career, he would not have lived long enough to have so positively impacted the lives of bodybuilders all over the world.

Mike Mentzer—a true hero of bodybuilding.

A GENUINE HERO

In the 1930s, Pulitzer Prize–winning philosopher and historian Will Durant made the comment that:

> Of the many ideals which in youth gave life a meaning and radiance missing from the chilly perspectives of middle age, one at least has remained with me as bright and satisfying as ever before—the shameless worship of heroes. In an age that would level everything and reverence nothing, I take my stand with Victorian Carlyle, and light my candles, like Mirandola before Plato's image, at the shrines of great men. . . . For why should we stand reverent before waterfalls and mountain tops, or a summer moon on a quiet sea, and not before the highest miracle of all—a man who is both great and good?

Apart from being a close friend, I have long considered Mike Mentzer to be a genuine hero, a man who, indeed, was both "great and good." Mentzer was a man who summated physical perfection in the world of bodybuilding, becoming one of the greatest bodybuilders of all time (thus fulfilling part one of Dr. Durant's definition); and a man who constantly sought honesty rather than reputation, integrity rather than commercialism, and truth above all. That this is evidence of the "good" (the second part of Dr. Durant's definition) should not need further elaboration.

Sadly, the world of bodybuilding has never possessed the same love for the heroic as Dr. Durant. To wit, for possessing the three virtues cited above, Mentzer was sorely punished: for the first he was condemned by the bodybuilding orthodoxy; for the second he was excommunicated from its power base; and for the third he would be denied the greatest title in bodybuilding along with the opportunity to earn a living from his passion.

These were hurdles that would have broken a less heroic spirit. Mentzer, however, would persevere and in time earn prestigious titles of a different sort (and of far greater worth in the arena of life); he would become known as "a fully actualized human being"; "a man of self-made soul"; "a pioneer in exercise science"; and (perhaps the one of which he was most proud) "a philosopher of mind and body."

In the mid 1970s when bodybuilding was just starting to become fashionable, Mentzer, like a breath—no, a cyclone—of fresh air, whistled through its murky and pungent halls, decimating myths and exploding falsehoods. In time, he built quite a following among seekers of truth within the bodybuilding community. Mentzer's well-reasoned conclusions, based for the first time upon logical thinking and scientific evidence rather than sales of supplements and equipment, brought bodybuilding out of its self-imposed dark ages and into the world of modern technology.

Attending this renaissance was a revolution in the way bodybuilding was performed and bodybuilders were perceived. Mentzer's articles (at that time—he would refine them in the years that followed) stated that one should never train more than 45 minutes per workout nor exercise more than four days per week. This at a time when Arnold Schwarzenegger and most other bodybuilders were training twice a day for up to two hours per workout and heading to the gym six days per week. Such a proposition would have been laughed out of consideration had it been advanced by anyone other than Mike Mentzer—whose string of contest victories (including the first-ever perfect score in the history of the Mr. Universe contest) was living testimony to the efficacy of his new training approach. In addition to his phenomenal physique was the fact that Mentzer was strikingly handsome and—a first for a professional bodybuilder—an intellectual. Here, finally, was the embodiment of the ancient Greek and Roman ideal of *mens sana in corpore sano*—a healthy mind in a healthy body.

Madison Avenue was quick to take advantage of this anomaly; by 1979 Mentzer had a bestselling poster, an agent, three bestselling books, and had appeared on numerous television shows, such as "Merv Griffin" and the ABC "Superstars" competition, in which he competed successfully against the greatest athletes in the world, demonstrating that not all

Mentzer was the embodiment of the ancient Greek ideal of "a healthy mind in a healthy body."

bodybuilders were muscle-bound and ineffective athletically. Many people of bodybuilding fame believe that the petty powers that controlled bodybuilding then became jealous and conspired to plot his downfall. And so it came to pass that in Sydney, Australia, at the 1980 Mr. Olympia competition, Mentzer, who was the odds-on favorite to win (and with good reason; he had come in 10 pounds of muscle heavier, more defined, and with a posing routine that those in attendance still talk about for its breathtaking impact and poignancy) would be relegated to fifth place.

After all, Mentzer had to be taught a lesson; he was becoming bigger than the sport itself, and his articles questioning the need for nutritional supplements—which were the very lifeblood of the commercial bodybuilding establishment—along with his refusal to endorse fraudulent training practices for the sake of going along to get along, necessitated that he be brought down a peg or two—or five. (It is interesting to note, lest the reader think I'm being subjective here, that CBS Sports had gone to the expense of sending a camera crew halfway around the world to videotape the event for broadcast on television, but after Mentzer's incongruous placing, they decided not to broadcast it.)

But Mentzer stood tall. If this was how their premier competition was to be judged, he would have no part of their competitions; if this was their reward for intellectual integrity and commitment to discovering a better, more efficient way to train, then it was no reward at all. And as Mentzer would agree, since the real reward is in the achievement in health and physical conditioning for the individual practitioner rather than rewards from external authority sources, perhaps he had been heading down the wrong path to begin with.

VALIDATION

There is a saying that the problem inherent in climbing the ladder of success is that most would-be climbers discover too late in life that the ladder they've been climbing is up against the wrong wall. Fortunately for Mentzer he came to recognize that his ladder had been placed against the wrong wall early in his career. He resigned from the public eye and from the bodybuilding magazines—leaving behind a six-figure income and unprecedented popularity and exposure—to continue his search for truth and the ideal training method, now unencumbered by the demands and expectations of others.

Not that he was passively studying; rather he was testing new applications of his theory of high-intensity training upon thousands of personal clients that he had taken under his wing—and his discoveries would astound not only Mentzer but the entire world of exercise science. Maximum muscle size and strength increases, Mentzer established, were possible from workouts lasting only 12 minutes in length and performed but once every four to seven days! Such a proposition would have been laughable—had it not been for the results that Mentzer revealed, not only in himself but now in thousands of clients. Suddenly high-intensity training was a legitimate way to work out and a slew of new "authorities" wrote books revealing the secrets of "their" research into this revolutionary method of training—seldom was Mentzer mentioned, let alone acknowledged for his pioneering efforts.

In time the magazines implored him to write again, to share his wisdom with their readers. Imagine what he was offering! Twelve minutes a week to realize your full genetic potential in terms of muscle mass and strength! In bodybuilding imagery this was the death of the old orthodoxy of the bodybuilding establishment and a complete rebirth to an entirely new perspective—a true science of exercise. Bodybuilding had found its renaissance, which has continued unabated until the present day, and its fountainhead was Michael John Mentzer.

Soon luminaries such as Tony Robbins, CEOs of Fortune 500 companies, competitive bodybuilders, and men and women seeking to get into their best possible shape in the shortest possible time sought out Mentzer's advice. None of them asked whether or not he ever won the 1980 Mr. Olympia (few of them even knew what it was), yet all of them knew who Mike Mentzer was, and it was his knowledge and his principles they sought.

Always an individualist, Mentzer preferred to work on his own terms; he spoke to the public through his own website (mikementzer .com), published his own books, produced his own audiotapes, and forever cultivated his own garden. He never expected anyone to accept what he had to say because he was a former champion bodybuilder, nor did he ask anyone to follow what he recommended without question. He challenged his students (and now the reader) not so much to agree or disagree with him, but to think for themselves and grow from the experience.

A GENUINELY BENEVOLENT HUMAN BEING

Although Mike passed away at a young age (49), there can be no doubt that he lived a full and rewarding life. But that fact does not diminish the pain of his loss for his friends, fans, family, and cowriter. Mike was that rarest of creatures: a genuinely benevolent human being who cared deeply about people and went out of his way to help all who came into his circle. He did not keep much of the money he made throughout his life, not because he had lavish tastes, but because he was forever help-ing out those he encountered who couldn't pay their rent, needed money for food or to further their education, or had other needs that Mike chose to obviate by his largess.

WRITING THIS BOOK

I had known Mike for 22 years when I first suggested to him that I wanted to create a book that would represent the distilled wisdom of his 34 years in bodybuilding training, competi-tion, and philosophy. Mike was somewhat sur-prised but delighted nevertheless at the request, and for reasons that now seem prophetic, I set about writing the book with him even before McGraw-Hill had signed on to publish the title. Two weeks before his death, I sent Mike a copy of this manuscript via E-mail attachment, and he wrote back indicating how pleased he was with the book. Ironically, while two publishers had put out books of Mike's during the 1980s, both were written for the general fitness audi-ence, whereas Mike's audience and, indeed, his passion had always been with bodybuilding.

As a writer who is considered an authority by many people, by virtue of having co-created and innovated two training systems (*Static Contraction Training* and *Power Factor Training*—both published by Contemporary Books), I have to acknowledge the influence that Mentzer has had on my own thinking in regards to both exercise science and on a some-what higher plane, philosophy. Were it not for Mentzer's influence (and at times mentorship), I would not have had the mindset to question bodybuilding tradition and to seek a better way. I have Mentzer to thank for this lesson—and for the lesson that bodybuilding is but an adjunct to a better life and not the reason for one's life.

My contribution to the creation of this book has been to its structure—not its content, as that is entirely Mike Mentzer's achievement. While we worked together on the manuscript for several months (with the help of Objec-tivist philosophy and our own knowledge of exercise physiology), we determined that the fundamental principles of the science of body-building were not three—intensity, duration, and frequency—as had long been asserted, but actually seven, and that only by fully under-standing these seven principles could one then be said to have a grasp of bodybuilding sci-ence. Mike's authority was final in all matters in regard to this book.

My work on this book was also an official tip of the hat to the life, career, beliefs, and example of Mike Mentzer; to my mind one of the greatest bodybuilders who ever lived. I say "greatest" not because he won so many titles, but because he built one of the greatest physiques of all time without once selling out; without once ever wavering from his belief in what is true and good; and because he refused to sell the public anything but his own integrity.

Each decade brings with it a new crop of champions, but they are quickly forgotten when the next crop of champions are harvested. Mentzer endures because he stood for something more—that there are some prin-ciples worth espousing even when great per-sonal cost is at stake. And in so doing, Mentzer revealed the potential inherent in all of us to actualize ourselves as human beings and to live fuller, more purposeful lives. One can't ask much more than this from one's heroes.

ACKNOWLEDGMENTS—AND A CONFESSION

It is never an easy process to lose a teacher. It is harder still to lose a close friend. When you lose both at once, the psyche protects itself by administering a form of cognitive anesthesia, which numbs the pain and allows one to pro-ceed with life. It was therefore a bittersweet experience putting the finishing touches on this book. The text was completed prior to Mike's passing, based upon his 20-plus years of expe-rience with and writing about the art, science, sport, and lifestyle of bodybuilding. This part was an absolute joy; I looked forward to each day on the job, knowing that I would be spend-ing time with my friend and mentor.

Mike Mentzer—perhaps the greatest bodybuilder of all time.

The hard part came when I was selecting the photographs for this book after Mike's death, for it was then that it hit me that this would be the *last* time we would ever hear from Mike Mentzer; it was no longer a bodybuilding book but, indeed, his final communiqué. That revelation hit hard and I found myself dragging the process out; I needed to see more photographs, make better selections, and make sure the book was the best I could possibly make it. I also, perhaps subconsciously, felt that as long as I didn't concede that the book was finished, there was still a book by Mike Mentzer to come.

The realities of publishing, however, gently but correctly reminded me that an agreement had been made by both Mike and me to submit the finished book and that the time had come to honor that agreement. And so with a heavy heart I completed the photo selection and captions. The photographs are quite simply—and objectively—the best shots ever taken of Mike Mentzer, and they were contributed by people who work for competing magazines but who came together for this project because they were his friends and wanted his last book to be a fitting tribute to a man they remembered with fondness and respect.

I am indebted to John Balik of *Ironman* magazine, who supplied the bulk of the photos that appear in this book; he knew Mike longer than almost anyone in bodybuilding and was there all through Mike's career—from his amateur days to his final months on earth. Along the way, John took some of the best physique shots of Mike ever to grace a roll of film and—without question—he captured the absolute best in-the-gym training shots of Mike actually working out when he was training to build muscle for competition. These are not posed photographs such as you see in most bodybuilding magazines and books written on the subject; these are the genuine article; the sweat is real, the weights are real, and the effort is bona fide "high intensity" (heavy duty) all the way. This is real bodybuilding; and Balik perfectly captured on film how real muscle is stimulated to grow bigger and stronger.

I also need to thank John's business partner, the renowned photographer Mike Neveux, whose eye has an uncanny knack of being able to focus precisely on what is important in a bodybuilding shot. His portrait shots and his in-the-gym workout shots are as near to perfection as is humanly possible.

Bob and Gail Gardner must also be singled out. Their photographs of Mike Mentzer were (and remain) legendary within the sport of bodybuilding; our cover shot is a result of their artistic genius, and the physique studies that grace many of the pages of this book are the direct result of their talent. Their "Hercules" shot of Mike, which opens Part VI, is perhaps the most famous physique study photograph in the history of bodybuilding.

Despite my being on a very tight budget, all of these artists opened their files and went to great personal expense and trouble to be part of Mike's final book. I know that Mike would be deeply touched by their benevolence and their friendship.

Finally, I need to single out Joanne Sharkey; Jo was Mike's business partner for many years and remains his most dedicated and loyal supporter. Above all this, however, she was Mike's friend; her kindness to Mike over the many years in which life was not kind to him, as well as her warm and positive support of this project, have endeared her to me as a human being of exceptional compassion, integrity, and honesty. I know that Mike would want Joanne acknowledged, as he acknowledged her repeatedly to me throughout his final days.

This then is the last testament of Michael John Mentzer, representing his final word on bodybuilding in all of its many facets.

For now, I will close this preface by stating with that old philosopher Seneca that "life, if thou knowest how to use it, is long enough." That Mike knew how to use it, surely, cannot ever be in doubt.

—John Little

"It is only within the context of having properly developed your mind that you will be able to truly enjoy the achievement of your material values, including that of a more muscular body."—Mike Mentzer

INTRODUCTION
A NEW PERSPECTIVE

Victor Hugo once said, "Nothing in this world is so powerful as an idea whose time has come." This idea arises from the rationalist philosophy that certain possibilities of thought must, out of logical necessity, appear in time when certain social, scientific, and psychological conditions have been fulfilled.

Judging by the response that my tapes, videos, and articles have received, along with the overwhelming acceptance of my revolutionary training approach at various bodybuilding seminars I've conducted all over the world, it might be safe to say that the time for the ideas contained herein has not only arrived, but is long overdue.

Most of the material contained within these pages is based on empirically validated data—some dating back to the nineteenth century—and that which is not will be simple self-evident fact that no reasonable person would deny. I have also dedicated a large portion of my adult life to seeking—and finally discovering—the fundamental principles of proper (i.e., high-intensity) bodybuilding exercise and arranging them in their proper hierarchical structure in order to reveal the very real integration between the mind and body when it comes to building strength and muscle mass.

The question of just what is the best way to train for rapid increases in muscular size and strength has been controversial and fraught with diverse opinion for much too long now. This book is intended for the serious bodybuilder who is fed up with opinion and is looking for something more concrete.

It is my sincere belief that this method of bodybuilding is a system and, as such, can be learned by anyone. If the reader spends enough time mastering the logically arranged sequence of topics in this book, he or she can grasp my approach to high-intensity training thoroughly enough to be able to answer his own training problems and become his or her own coach and trainer.

It has been more than two decades since I have departed from bodybuilding tradition with my radically different approach to training and diet. And while I've always possessed a broad awareness of the singular logical standard that guided me in my new approach, my own knowledge has grown exponentially over the past six years (since I made a dedicated and passionate attempt to better understand the role of logic in human thought and of the philosophical primaries of "the Law of Identity" and the "Law of Causality," and then tested my new bodybuilding theories on thousands of bodybuilders the world over). The end result of this period of growth has resulted in a certainty in matters where before only approximations were possible. This is not to suggest that I was always this certain. I well recall my

Muscle magazines exist primarily to sell products, not to dispense valid training information.

first seminar as a professional bodybuilder; though I knew I had something of worth to offer those attending the seminar, I wasn't sure I could present the material in a way that would be meaningful.

Fortunately, as things turned out, that initial seminar proved very successful, with the majority of those attending convinced that they had learned something new and valuable, and that I had provided them with a totally new perspective regarding the whole field of bodybuilding. Subsequent seminars witnessed a polishing and refinement of my subject material. Over the past 20 years I've conducted thousands of bodybuilding seminars— probably more than any other top bodybuilder —and a large part of their success can be

attributed to the fact that I don't expect anyone to accept anything that I have to say just because I've won a couple of top titles. There exists no direct correlation between an individual's degree of muscular development and his scientific knowledge of bodybuilding. I've always reasoned that if the material I presented was valid in and of itself, was offered in a logical manner, and was designed to appeal to one's reason and common sense, then the likelihood of it being accepted for its intrinsic worth was greater.

I typically tell my students in high-intensity training that the first step towards gaining a more realistic perspective on the sport of bodybuilding is to look at the various influences responsible for shaping our current

Mentzer made a systematic study of exercise and stress physiology along with nutritional science and applied the findings to the needs of the bodybuilder.

outlook. More than any other source, the muscle magazines have shaped our views and attitudes regarding bodybuilding. With virtually no other source of information, bodybuilders have had to turn to the muscle magazines as their one source of reliable information. What many fail to keep in mind, however, is that these are primarily commercial publications; their primary reason for existence is to sell products, not to dispense scientific bodybuilding information. If you look somewhere below the masthead of most muscle publications, you'll find stated something to the

effect that their publication is "devoted to the science of bodybuilding."

If these muscle magazines are indeed scientific journals, then who, may I ask, are the scientists on their editorial staffs or among the writers they employ? That's right, there usually are none! These magazines are commercial entities first and foremost; in fact, they are registered with the government as catalogues. Now this is not meant to suggest that these muscle magazines serve no worthwhile purpose. They do inspire young and upcoming bodybuilders, but while they occasionally do dispense valid training advice, it is so often lost in the reams of conflicting opinions and outright nonsense published in some of them, that the valid information is rendered useless.

This is not to say that there doesn't exist a coherent body of scientific data and principles regarding bodybuilding. The problem is that most of the scientific knowledge regarding bodybuilding has been published piecemeal by diverse authors in a wide variety of texts, many of them highly technical physiology studies, with the result that much of this information never filters down to those who could make the best practical use of it—the bodybuilders. The bodybuilder therefore has always had to rely on logically suspect opinion coming from other bodybuilders and the commercially biased hype sold through the muscle publications.

What I have to offer you in this book is a new perspective on bodybuilding, based not on transient opinion and commercial considerations, but one derived from scientific research and sound thinking. And, no, this book is not a promise of a 20-inch arm or a Mr. America physique. That is something that no one, and no training method, can honestly offer. What follows is a system of thought that, when properly applied to your training, will enable you to develop your muscles to the limits of your genetically programmed potential faster and more efficiently than any other system presently known.

Mentzer displaying the results of his logical and scientific approach to bodybuilding.

Part I

PRELIMINARY CONSIDERATIONS

Mentzer built his muscula[r]
mass slowly but steadily [over]
a period of many years.

Chapter 1

THE ROLE OF REALISTIC GOALS

Those readers who have been engaged in serious bodybuilding for more than a year probably have realized that the growth of muscle tissue beyond normal levels is a relatively slow process. And while I have never seen the results of studies that might reveal exactly how many pounds the average bodybuilder gains in the course of one year of hard training, I think that most experienced bodybuilders would agree that a five-pound gain of *pure* muscle tissue—as opposed to five pounds of body weight, despite its composition—would be considered a considerable achievement.

Five pounds of muscle tissue may not sound very impressive, but if a bodybuilder were able to sustain that rate of growth (5 pounds of *pure* muscle tissue per year) for five years, he would, at the end of that period, end up some 25 pounds of muscle heavier. If you could envision that much beefsteak laid out in front of you on the dinner table, you would then get some idea as to just how much "meat" 25 pounds of muscle is—enough to transform the average American male weighing 155 pounds into a veritable Hercules at 180 pounds

of solid, cut-up muscle. It should also be remembered that of that average American male's 155 pounds of body weight, the muscle weight component is roughly 20 pounds (the remainder being bone, water, fat, and waste materials). Given this fact, his muscle weight gain of 25 pounds over five years would represent a transformation that would more than double his existing muscle mass!

Considering that the majority of the top muscle stars past and present weigh less than 200 pounds, that really is quite an achievement. I recall that at the 1977 Mr. Olympia contest bodybuilding luminaries such as Frank Zane weighed in at 187 pounds; Bill Grant at 184 pounds; Boyer Coe tipped the scales at a mere 196 pounds; and Ed Corney competed at a weight of 174 pounds. Barring the odd genetic freak, you'd actually be hard-pressed to find more than a handful of top bodybuilding competitors in contest shape that would weigh in excess of 200 pounds.

One of the most massively muscled bodybuilders from that era was Danny Padilla, a man who won the Mr. Universe title in Nimes,

France, weighing a very muscular and cut-up 165 pounds. I recall Danny telling me that when he first began training 10 years prior to that contest he weighed a meager 120 pounds. That represents a gain of 45 pounds spanning a 10-year training career, with the yearly average gain being 4½ pounds. Those figures may offer hope to those of you disappointed with similar gains.

Bearing this in mind it is now evident just how ludicrous some of those commercial claims in bodybuilding magazines are—such as those promising "a pound a day" of muscle gain if you take a particular nutritional supplement. There was even one well-known top bodybuilder who promised those purchasing his training courses that they would "gain 100 pounds of muscle" if they followed the advice contained in his booklets. It is doubtful that he ever succeeded in gaining that much muscle in his entire career—and yet he was promising everyone else in the world just that.

Of course there will be a number of you reading this book that cannot be counted in the ranks of the average. A few might possess well-above-average potential in gaining muscle mass at a rapid rate—a potential that will enable you to add up to 10 or more pounds of muscle tissue in a one-year period. But even these unusual few, whose abundance of the required genetic factors will allow for such rapid growth, won't see the results of such growth every time they step onto a scale. The individual whose potential allows him to gain a solid 12 pounds of muscle a year won't see those results on a day-to-day basis, or even a weekly one; most body weight scales just aren't sensitive enough to record fractions of a pound. Only if he were to gain at a steady rate of a pound per month for 12 months might he witness a weight gain once a month. Then there may be a month or two interspersed through the year when he makes no gains at all, but then proceeds to his 12 pound yearly

Mentzer *(left)* and Casey Viator *(right)* clowning for the camera; both men possessed a superabundance of the genetic gifts required to become champion bodybuilders.

gain by adding 2 pounds of muscle some other month. It is a rare individual indeed who makes such steady gains that they'll show up the same each and every month for a year. The majority will find that they gain in cycles: i.e., three months may pass with no visible signs of improvement, and then the next month their size and strength skyrockets. These growth patterns are highly individual, and thus will vary broadly from person to person.

It will be these few blessed individuals possessing all the required genetic factors who might possibly reach the top and take the big titles. (The next chapter will delve more deeply into the role of genetics in assessing one's ultimate potential.)

I stated at the outset that this book was not intended as a guarantee of a Mr. America physique. Nor would I insult your intelligence and tell you that by following the advice contained in these pages you'll end up gaining 50 or 100 pounds of muscle. The material contained in this chapter was not meant to frustrate you either, but to show just how difficult

and slow the acquisition of a top physique might be. And if I was successful in doing that, you'll probably realize for yourself the utter absurdity of training six days a week for up to 25 hours per week. Can you really justify 1,200 hours per year of your time and energy gaining a couple of pounds of muscle? Especially when you discover how you may have been selling yourself short—vastly underestimating your growth potential—when you actually had the capability of gaining 8 pounds of muscle a year from a tiny fraction of the total amount of training. In many cases, the unbridled enthusiasm that leads to training excesses is the very thing that slows down the progress of the majority of bodybuilders—frustrating indeed.

Think of what could be accomplished were you to channel 1,200 hours of your time and energy each year to making a million dollars or the attaining of a college degree—why, you'd likely be on your way to your first million by now and probably have affixed a couple of Ph.D.s to your name.

Mentzer cultivated many interests outside of bodybuilding, including the creation of a very successful mail-order business.

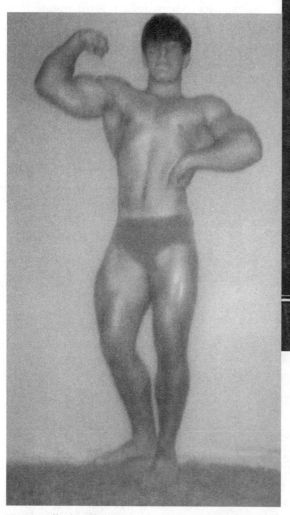

Mentzer displayed good potential for building muscle even when 15 years old, reaching an all-time peak by the time he competed in the 1980 Mr. Olympia contest 14 years later.

Chapter 2

INDIVIDUAL POTENTIAL

After having read the previous chapter, many of you are probably asking yourselves this question: how can I know just what my potential for developing large muscles is? Unfortunately, there exists no surefire method for accurately assessing an individual's ultimate potential. There are certain traits, however, that suggest to the aspiring bodybuilder just where he might be headed.

Individuals inherit characteristics peculiar to their parents and not common to the species as a whole such as facial appearance, hair color, and blood type. These characteristics are fixed in the individual and not subject to progressive alteration. Other inherited characteristics such as intelligence and physical size are not fixed, and they can thus be altered from the outside.

The genes (hereditary material within a cell) responsible for mature body size can't find expression in an individual deprived of adequate nutrients during the early stages of maturation and growth. The very same applies to the full development of a person's intellect; deprived of early intellectual stimulation, a person's intellect will not develop very far, even

if the hereditary material for it is present. These environmental influences are necessary for the development of normal levels of physical size and intelligence and for the development of above-normal levels—levels beyond those required for the carrying out of tasks involved in day-to-day living—of size and intellect; a person must expose himself to demands and the performance of tasks greater than those encountered in the course of daily living. In the case of developing larger than normal muscle size, a person must expose his muscles to progressively increasing levels of high-intensity training. And in the case of developing a superior intellect, a person must regularly attempt increasingly complex mental tasks. Improvements never result in either case merely by repeating things that are already easy.

While it is true that anyone can improve upon his or her existing levels of muscular size or intellect by following the advice mentioned above, in all cases limits will exist and there is yet no means by which mankind can transcend them. (Soon this may change as genetic engineers continue to unravel the mysteries of the DNA molecule.)

Along with certain psychological factors necessary in pursuing a goal to its fulfillment, there are definite inherited traits that represent the single most important consideration in building a championship physique. While anyone can improve upon his starting level of development, only a select few will become top champions, and these are the ones with the greatest abundance of the required inherited physical characteristics.

These characteristics offer the aspiring bodybuilder a guide to where he is headed—and indicate areas that may require greater attention during training.

SOMATOTYPE

While an infinite variety of body types exist, authorities have concluded that there are three readily identifiable types that recur most often. Dr. W. H. Sheldon categorized an individual's body by analyzing the degree to which each of the three types was present. He called his system somatotyping.

The three somatotypic variables are endomorphy, mesomorphy, and ectomorphy.

Mentzer *(left)* was pure mesomorph.

- Endomorphy refers to the tendency toward soft round body contours. A typical endomorph is squat, having a round torso, thick neck, and short, fat legs and arms.
- Mesomorphy refers to the tendency toward being muscular. A mesomorph is built square and strong, having broad muscular shoulders, powerful chest and limbs, and carrying little bodyfat.
- Ectomorphy refers to the tendency toward linearity or slimness. Ectomorphs are usually tall and always thin in the torso and limbs. They carry little bodyfat or muscle.

SKELETAL FORMATION

In assessing an individual's predisposition towards building a championship physique, it is essential to consider bodily proportions, which are determined by the length, thickness, and ratio of a person's bones.

The bodily proportions normally associated with the ideal bodybuilding physique are broad shoulders, narrow hips, and arms and legs of medium length. Bodybuilding legends Sergio Oliva (from the 1960s) and Steve Reeves (from the 1940s) are excellent examples of how well-balanced proportions can benefit a bodybuilder.

While bones must be large enough to support a heavy musculature, they can't be too large. Otherwise they'll obliterate the beautiful lines that are the hallmark of the bodybuilder's physique.

MUSCLE LENGTH

While skeletal size and formation enable an individual to support massive muscle structures, the ultimate size a muscle might develop to is actually dictated primarily by its length. In other words, a muscle's length dictates its thickness: its width will never exceed its length, otherwise it would be unable to contract. A biceps muscle that is one inch long will never

Genetic potential varies across a broad continuum.

be more than one inch thick, or one that is two inches long, two inches thick, and so on. The bone to which the muscle is attached is of no great significance—instead it is the length from the tendon attachment at one end of the muscle to the tendon attachment at the other end that determines how much mass a muscle will appear to have.

However, a bodybuilder with short biceps does not necessarily possess short muscles throughout her body. The length of any specific muscle seems to be a random feature within any given bodybuilder's musculature, with differences usually existing from one side of the body to the other and from one bodypart to the next. It is the extremely rare person who has uniform muscle length and/or size over his entire body.

"It is the length from the tendon attachment at one end of the muscle to the tendon attachment at the other end that determines how much mass a muscle will have."—Mike Mentzer

Muscular definition also is largely determined by your genetic heritage.

FAT DISTRIBUTION

Just as people are genetically programmed to increase the size of certain muscles, they also inherit a certain number of fat or adipose cells. The distribution of these cells is genetically determined as well. The average nonobese person possesses approximately 25 to 30 billion fat cells, the moderately obese about 50 billion and the very obese as many as 240 billion. This wide range may help explain why some people find it a near impossibility to keep fat off permanently.

Racial and geographic background determines in large part where fat is deposited. People from colder parts of the world, like Germany and Norway, have much of their fat distributed in the abdomen and torso areas, which helps insulate the internal organs from the extreme cold and maintain a steady core temperature. People from warm areas, such as Africa, naturally tend to store less fat subcutaneously in order to allow body heat to escape, thus maintaining a cool body. These types store more fat internally and in the area of the buttocks from where it can be mobilized more

Muscle fiber density—the amount of fibers within a given cross section of muscle—determines the mass potential of a muscle.

readily for energy in times of privation and/or famine.

Modern man's exposure to extreme temperatures has been enormously minimized with central heating and air conditioning. Despite that fact, researchers have documented proof that civilized man is programmed for fat deposition by blueprints laid down by his forebears of the Ice Age. Nevertheless, given the criteria by which we judge the modern bodybuilder, the darker races tend to have an advantage in terms of leanness and extreme muscular definition.

FIBER DENSITY AND NEUROLOGICAL EFFICIENCY

Somatotype, skeletal formation, muscle length, and fat distribution are genetic traits that are more or less visible and therefore ascertainable to a high degree of accuracy. However, muscle fiber density and neurological efficiency—two inherited features that play a role in determining ultimate potential—are invisible. Estimates of the amount of muscle fibers within a given volume, or cross-sectional area, of a specific muscle can only be approximated through biopsies.

Fiber density, like muscle length, determines the mass potential of a muscle. The more fibers per given volume of muscle, the thicker that muscle's potential to develop. Nevertheless, rather than attempting to procure such an expensive medical procedure, give your training some time to see how rapidly your muscles thicken.

Neurological efficiency refers to the relationship between the nervous system and the muscles. How nerves innervate the muscles and how they are activated by the brain determine the degree of muscle power and the number of fibers required to produce a certain movement against a certain resistance. People with high levels of neurological efficiency have the ability to contract a greater percentage of fibers during a maximal effort. In an all-out effort the average person may contract 30 percent of the fibers within a specific muscle. A few people

No matter what your genetic potential, you can still improve your levels of muscle mass and strength by training with high intensity.

may have the capacity to activate as many as 40 percent, while a blessed few may manage 50 percent. The ability to contract a high percentage of fibers increases contractile capacity, thus enabling more intense exertion. In terms of endurance this is a disadvantage, but a great advantage for stimulating growth or single attempt efforts.

INNATE ADAPTABILITY

We've all witnessed the Sisyphean efforts of the zealot who seems to train harder than anyone we've ever seen, yet never shows any visible signs of improvement, or two individuals who follow the same training protocol and while one makes good progress, gaining in strength and size seemingly with every workout, the other appears to be making no progress at all. Since genetically mediated traits such as height, sunlight stress tolerance, and intelligence are expressed across a broad continuum, it occurred to me several years back that the ability of the human body to tolerate the stress of exercise (particularly high-intensity exercise), being a genetically mediated feature, would likewise be expressed across a broad continuum. Even a casual observation will reveal

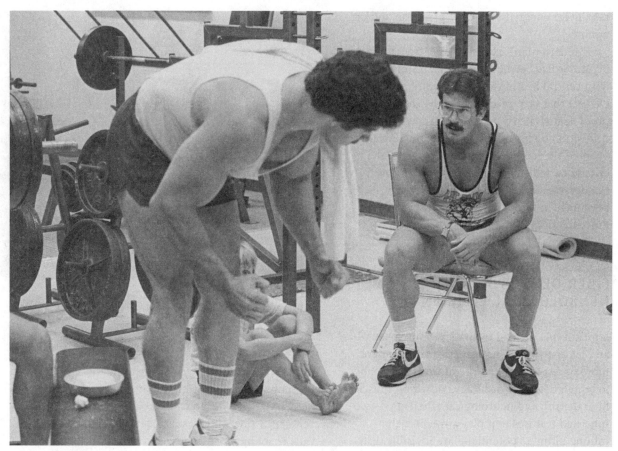

Mentzer *(right)* discusses a point about proper Olympic weightlifting technique with fellow bodybuilder Lou Ferrigno *(left)* as the two prepare to compete in ABC television's "The Superstars Competition."

that, with regard to height, there are tall people at one extreme and small people at the other; with regard to sunlight stress tolerance, there are light-skinned people who burn easily (including those genetic anomalies known as albinos) and dark-skinned people who can spend hours in direct sunlight with little to no burning at all; similarly with intelligence there are those with low, almost nonexistent IQs at one extreme and genius IQs at the other. And, of course, there are almost as many variants within the gradation of high to low as there are individuals. A similar situation exists with regard to one's genetic ability to tolerate (and respond to) the stress of exercise. Exercise is a form of stress to the body much like the stress of ultraviolet light is. Just where in the continuum of innate adaptability to exercise stress each individual will fall is mediated by their genetic predisposition to tolerate and adapt to the stress of high-intensity exercise. If one can

adapt quickly, then the opportunity to train a little more frequently will be possible (whether it would be desirable, however, is another question that I will address later in this book); whereas if one falls somewhere on the other side of the continuum, it would be impossible for him to tolerate and adapt to frequent training sessions and would be better to take such stress in moderate doses and infrequently. I will go into this component in greater detail later in the book, because, of the traits just listed, an awareness of this factor permits you a range within which to manipulate it.

For the moment it is important to keep in mind that limits will always exist and as these limits are probably of a genetic nature, there is little we can do to alter them. So, if you have made an honest assessment of your potential and realize that you are limited, don't despair. As a person's potential is something that can only be accurately assessed in retrospect, you'll never really know what you might achieve unless you train hard and go on to realize that potential. When Arnold Schwarzenegger started training at age fifteen, he had no way of knowing what his future held. It was an unrelenting drive and ambition that made him achieve so much in the sport of bodybuilding.

PSYCHOLOGICAL FACTORS

Those of you who train in commercial or public gyms with other bodybuilders have undoubtedly encountered those who obviously possess extraordinary physical potential, yet never seem to go as far in the sport as they might. More often than not, this can be directly attributed to a paucity of the required psychological factors needed to develop a top-notch physique. While the world is teeming with untold numbers of genetic anomalies in possession of a motherlode of all the necessary traits for building large muscles, the incidence of those exceptional individuals also in possession of the necessary ambition and intelligence needed to actualize their potential is much less.

Given a representative cross section of 100,000 normal males, there might be 20 from that number who have an extraordinary physical potential for developing a muscular physique. Of those 20 thoroughbreds, perhaps five with the drive and determination required to take up the hard training for the length of time needed will be able to actualize a good percentage of their potential. The number will be small because it requires an obsessed nature to pursue any endeavor to its limit. To go on and come up with someone from those obsessed five with enough intelligence to discover what is actually required to realize his potential will prove more difficult since such traits as ambition and intelligence are less tangible than physical ones.

How does a person go about cultivating the psychological traits necessary to develop a great physique? Again, a certain amount of intelligence is inherited while another portion is determined by environmental influences. Don't allow yourself to become that one-dimensional type of individual whose entire existence revolves around the gym and training. You will never increase your knowledge of exercise physiology and nutrition by looking at pictures of your favorite muscle stars all day. Broaden and diversify your interests to include things other than bodybuilding. This will aid in deepening and broadening your mind, which will help you to keep your new perspective on bodybuilding in sight and in proper focus.

While there may be things you can practice to increase your drive, I feel it rests with the individual to cultivate that germ of ambition that lies within all of us. Only a very tiny minority make it to the top in any arena of endeavor, and it's usually those who want it the most.

Mentzer remained an avid reader throughout his lifetime—philosophy, psychology, and the novels of Ayn Rand being his favorites—but he also read the news intensely in order to keep abreast of the goings-on in the world outside of the gym.

Two titans of bodybuilding: bodybuilding champion Mike Mentzer *(left)* and publisher Joe Weider *(right)* held two opposing views of bodybuilding; Weider recommended through his magazine that bodybuilders train up to four hours a day for six days a week, whereas Mentzer believed that anything more than the precise amount required was a waste of time.

Chapter 3

ON THE NEED FOR PRINCIPLES

The commercial bonanza that the bodybuilding and fitness market enjoys has led to a long line of self-proclaimed authorities and experts. The result has been a ceaseless profusion of information that no one, including the purveyors of such information along with those for whom it is intended, has been willing or able to interpret.

Long on hype and short on facts, the modern bodybuilding authorities have left aspiring bodybuilders bewildered and without rational guidance. As a consequence, they are endangering the future of their own market.

The notion that bodybuilding is a science has been written and talked about by top bodybuilders, certain exercise physiologists, and muscle magazine writers for decades. However, before it can qualify as a legitimate, practical applied science, bodybuilding must have a consistent, rational theoretical base, something that none of the aforementioned has ever attempted to provide. In fact, what passes today for the so-called science of modern bodybuilding is little more than a collection of random, disconnected, and contradictory ideas

culled from the observations of champion bodybuilders and interpreted and written about by magazine writers. The latter are individuals whose job it is to write articles, not painstakingly interpret information and integrate factual data. This latter quality requires an intimate familiarity with and ability to effectively employ the discipline of logic.

Many of these authorities have even alleged that there are no objective, universal principles of productive exercise, claiming that since each bodybuilder is unique, every individual bodybuilder requires a different training program. This implies that the issue of what is the best way to build muscle is a subjective one, only to be resolved by arbitrary means, random motions, and blind urges. Unfortunately, under such conditions bodybuilding is not and cannot be considered a science, as science is an exacting discipline based on and guided by objective principles derived from well-authenticated facts.

Despite their belief that no universal principles exist and that each bodybuilder requires a different training program, many of these

Mike Mentzer—champion of the scientific method of bodybuilding.

themselves are basing their position on a principle—that "more is better." Presumably this is an ethical/economic principle: more money, more success, more love, more self-esteem, more values would seem to us as being better than less of the same. However, taking a principle from one context, such as economics, and applying it uncritically and blindly to another context—bodybuilding in this case—is to commit the logical fallacy of context switching, and in this instance, lacking both consistency and a factual base, such a position raises more questions than it answers—such as:

- If more sets or exercise is better, why stop at 12 to 20 sets? Wouldn't 75 to 100 sets (or more) be preferable?
- Why the contradiction? If everyone is different and if each bodybuilder requires a different routine, why do these authorities advocate the same number of sets for everyone?
- Why the equivocation? Whose word should we take? Who is telling the truth: the advocates of 12 to 20 or the advocates of 75 to 100? (Or are they both unintentionally relating a falsehood?)
- Why the lack of exactitude? Will a bodybuilder obtain equal results from 12 sets and 14 sets and 20 sets, or from 75 sets and 87 sets and 100 sets?
- Why the evasion? Are all of the recommended sets to be performed with the same degree of intensity of effort by the same individuals all of the time?

Where can a confused aspiring bodybuilder expect to find the answers to these and other pressing questions? I well recall the response offered me from one of these authorities (in fact, the former editor-in-chief of one of the leading bodybuilding magazines): "Each bodybuilder has to be his own scientific agent and find the routine that works best for him." Interesting. Such an answer appeals to our sense of individuality—but what if a particular bodybuilder isn't a very good scientist or lacks the background to assess the facts in a rational or meaningful way? The authority had no answer to that question.

same people advocate that bodybuilders should perform 12 to 20 sets per bodypart for at least two hours per session. For best gains the experts advise that the trainee should perform two, even three, sessions per day six days a week, with the seventh day off—for sabbath, presumably. And while they decry the use of a "principled approach" to bodybuilding, they

On occasion a bodybuilding authority will cite the success of certain bodybuilding champions who have trained using the "more is better" principle. At my seminars and in conversations with various gym members throughout the world, bodybuilders who have fallen under the influence of such authorities will ask me, "If 12 to 20 sets is not the right way to train, how do you account for the success of so many of the bodybuilding champions—guys like Mr. Olympia winners Arnold Schwarzenegger and Lee Haney?" The answer is that while it's true that these champions do train in such a fashion, what goes unreported is that so too have all the failures; the thousands of bodybuilders who never grew one pound of muscle from such practices and who then gave up their physique aspirations and quit bodybuilding in a state of utter despair. The bodybuilding press doesn't report on these individuals.

Furthermore, all who have achieved extraordinary levels of muscular development (particularly top champions like Schwarzenegger and Haney) possessed an abundance of the requisite genetic traits, including long muscle bellies, greater-than-average muscle-fiber density, and superior innate adaptability. In addition, all of the top champs were fueled psychologically by an enormous passion that enabled them to train for protracted periods when they experienced little or no progress.

It should also be noted that a training method currently attributed to a champion bodybuilder is not necessarily the same one he's always used. In many cases the champs started their training careers and developed the bulk of their muscular mass with abbreviated routines performed two to three days a week using basic exercises and heavy weights. As they progressed into the competitive ranks, they increased the number of sets along with the number of workouts per week (you'll see why this is a mistake shortly and why it would explain why many reach a certain level and then stagnate and even retrogress). For certain bodybuilders, increasing the duration and frequency of their workouts was done in conjunction with the use of steroids, which help to prevent, or at least reduce, the loss of mass and

Mentzer openly challenged the bodybuilding orthodoxy to defend their training proclamations. Few were willing, and even fewer able, to respond to his challenge.

strength that otherwise would result from such marathon training sessions conducted over a period of time. This, of course, is the dirty little secret that the magazines don't let you in on. Not that I am without empathy; I too was once a victim of the "more is better" syndrome and believed that everybody but me had the answers to my bodybuilding questions.

When I began bodybuilding more than three decades back, I was so enthusiastic and desirous of building a physique such as that of my hero, Bill Pearl, that I was willing to do anything I thought necessary to achieve that goal. Had someone told me at that time that if I would work out every day for 12 hours I would end up looking like Bill Pearl by the time I was 40 years old, I wouldn't have taken the time to question him—I would've started my first 12-hour workout straightaway. Such was the nature of 12-year-old Mike Mentzer's enthusiasm—and ignorance.

From the time I started bodybuilding at the age of 12 until I was 15, I had actually trained in a relatively sensible and productive

It was only when Mentzer stopped training according to what he read in the muscle magazines that he started growing again.

manner (just how sensible and productive I was not to discover for a number of years). Along with the first set of weights that my dad had bought me came an instruction booklet that suggested beginners like myself work out no more than three days a week, performing three sets for each body part. That formula proved so successful that in those three years I went from an initial body weight of 95 pounds with 9-inch arms to a weight of 165 pounds and 15½-inch arms. Not bad for a 15-year-old kid!

It was at the age of 15 that I really began to take on the thick rounded muscular look of a bodybuilder. I can remember doing my sets of Preacher curls out in the backyard of my parents' home in Ephrata, Pennsylvania, on hot summer days and then running into my bedroom while my arms were still pumped so I could admire them. It was right around that

period I began to take seriously the notion that I might be Mr. America some day, and in retrospect, it was at that moment I began to misdirect my efforts.

I thought then that as my resolve to be a top bodybuilder had moved up a step, it was time to start training like other top bodybuilders. Since every single title winner was training six days a week for at least two hours a day, who was I to question such practices? These guys were my heroes, so I followed suit. For a young man of 15 with no real responsibilities and a superabundance of energy, such training didn't seem all that demanding. I noticed that my gains had slowed down considerably after beginning that type of marathon training, but then I was told, "Your gains are *supposed* to slow down as you progress."

It wasn't until four years later, while I was in the Air Force, that I began to question my

It was at Mentzer's *(left)* meeting with Casey Viator *(right)* at the 1971 Mr. America contest (both men were competitors) that Mike first learned of the high-intensity training approach. Here the two share a light moment in Gold's Gym, Venice, California, circa 1978.

training practices. By that time I had increased my training to more than three hours a day for six days a week, and noting how almost imperceptibly slow my gains were, I began to become concerned. I reasoned that if three hours a day in the gym weren't enough to make gains, then I would have to increase to four or five hours a day. That's what I had read most of the top bodybuilders in California were doing anyway. The only problem I had was one of resigning myself to the notion of being a gym rat. It wasn't so much that I couldn't justify spending that much time in the gym every day, rather than the fact that there just weren't enough hours a day that would allow me to do it! I was already feeling tired and drained from the effects of my 12-hour workdays in the Air

Force and the three-hour-a-day workouts. If developing a top physique meant giving up all of my social life and spending one-third of my waking hours in some dank gymnasium, I wasn't sure it was really worth it any more!

Agonizing over the prospect of having to forsake my dreams of ever being a top bodybuilder, I was fortunate enough at that time to make the acquaintance of Casey Viator, then the 1971 Mr. America. Casey was only 19 years old when he won the Mr. America title, but to my mind he was the best Mr. America we'd ever had. What made Casey's win even more interesting was that he was engaged in what at that time seemed to be a very unusual type of training. Unlike every other top bodybuilder—who were training for up to five hours every day—Casey was only training one hour a day with only three workouts a week! If Casey could develop a physique of his caliber with only three hours of training a week, it struck me that there was still hope that I too might win the Mr. America title some day.

My introduction to Casey and his methods of training back in 1971 served to rekindle my waning enthusiasm, and after a forced layoff from 1971 to 1974 because of a serious shoulder injury, I resumed contest training in earnest by the early part of 1975. Having whipped myself into good enough shape, I entered the 1975 Mr. America, placing third behind Robby Robinson and Roger Callard. I knew that in order to come back and win the America in 1976 I would have to improve considerably because the competition promised to be extremely tough, with Callard and Danny Padilla out for blood. As things turned out, I improved myself beyond my wildest expectations that year and went on to win the 1976 Mr. America, taking first on every judge's card!

Later, I would learn from Casey's mentor, Arthur Jones (the man who invented the Nautilus exercise machines that were all the rage throughout the '70s and '80s and himself one of the most knowledgeable people I've ever met with regard to muscle physiology), specific absolutes about human response to high-intensity stress exercise, specific principles that—once I understood and employed them—allowed me to reduce my training time

even more drastically and to increase my results beyond my wildest expectations. When I won the Mr. Universe contest in 1979 (with the only perfect score ever awarded in that competition) and the heavyweight Mr. Olympia title later that same year, I was training roughly 45 minutes per workout and engaging in only two to three workouts per week.

In the past two decades, I have learned even more about exercise science and detected even more fundamental principles that, when integrated with the exercise principles I learned from Jones, have resulted in my seldom advocating a workout that lasts longer than 10 minutes and that would have my clients in the gym no more than once a week. And, like me when I was training for serious competition, my clients are making gains in muscle size and strength with every set of every workout they perform.

How is it possible to make such outstanding progress with so little training? By training according to valid principles. For those frustrated bodybuilders who haven't given up; who refuse to allow the flame of their passion for a more muscular body to go out; who have some awareness of the role of facts, logic, and reason in their lives, let me assure you that there is a science of muscle building and that it can be understood by anyone willing to exercise the required effort to understand seven fundamental principles that, taken together, form the matrix of bodybuilding science.

When Mike Mentzer applied the principles of high-intensity training to his workouts he reduced his training time and increased his results beyond his wildest expectations.

Part II

FUNDAMENTALS

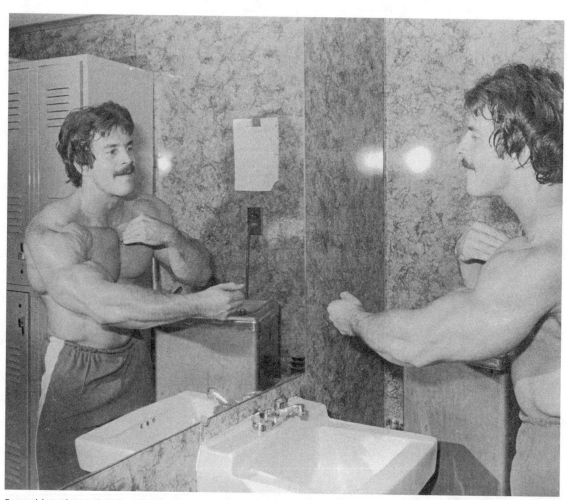

Everything that exists has an identity, a nature, including muscle tissue. Once you understand this, you can better direct your training efforts for superior development.

Chapter 4

THE FIRST PRINCIPLE
IDENTITY

A principle, properly defined, is a proposition that claims to be a correct description of some aspect of reality and/or a guide for successful human action. A principle can fulfill its proper intellectual function only if the proposition or propositions that make it up have precisely defined meanings—this is true of any principle or theory for that matter, whether it be the theory of relativity, the theory of evolution, or the theory of high-intensity training. The process of establishing precise definitions is rigorously demanding, but as definitions are the tools of thought, the better your tools, the better (i.e., the more precise, the closer to the facts of reality) your thinking will be. The improper use of principles, using them without knowing their exact definitions, is one of the primary causes of illogic, especially in the field of bodybuilding.

Let's look at the science of bodybuilding. Just as knowledge in the fields of mathematics and philosophy has a structure, so does the context of knowledge that constitutes the science of bodybuilding. And as such terms as "muscles," "development," "training," and

"strength" have specific definitions or denotations, so does our first principle, which is that of *identity*—the clear defining of our terms and the nature or properties inherent in those terms.

The principle of identity actually forms a triumvirate with two other concepts, *consciousness* and *existence*, which together are the axioms of any meaningful philosophy. In fact, they literally establish the base of all human knowledge. The foundation of reason and objectivity as held implicitly in every statement, proposition, fact, or bit of knowledge is the idea: I am conscious of something that exists, and everything that exists possesses identity or a "nature."

Philosophy itself can be said to be the intellectual discipline, the purpose of which is to discover the fundamental principles, or laws, underlying and governing the structure and actions of the entities that constitute the universe. This, in turn, is what enables the sciences to study specific, isolated aspects of reality, which for our purposes in this book will be the study of stimulating maximum muscle growth. Philosophy's discovery and explicit statement of the principle of identity, and its corollary, the principle called the Law of Causality, have provided human beings with the requisite intellectual base that made it possible for medicine, geology, physics, engineering, and all other sciences to flourish, including the science of bodybuilding.

"Bodybuilding science is based on an understanding of the universality of the principles of human anatomy and physiology." —Mike Mentzer

The principle of identity states that everything that exists (entities and their actions, qualities, attributes, and relationships) has an identity, a nature: that a thing is what it is and can be nothing else; or as Aristotle first posited it, "A is A." The principle of identity put into action affects the Law of Causality, or "cause-and-effect," which states that an entity can act only in accord with its nature and cannot act otherwise—which is why a rock cannot fly, a bird cannot conceptualize, and a muscle cannot grow without the imposition of the requisite stimulus.

Most bodybuilders make a single mistake, a fundamental mental error, which in turn is responsible for all their other training mistakes: they fail to recognize that bodybuilding is a part of exercise science, which flows from medical science. And that science is a discipline that absolutely requires man to use a specific method of thought (logic) to gain precise knowledge of reality so that he can successfully achieve his goals.

THE IDENTITY OF THE HUMAN BODY

That aspect of reality of most central concern and importance to human beings is, of course, human beings. And in order to survive and succeed in his fullest capacity as a human being, man must be able to identify his own nature (including his means of knowledge) as well as the nature of the world (or universe) in which he acts. And, remember, fundamentally a thing is what it is; we live in a universe where everything—including a human mind and body—has a specific, clear-cut identity and can be nothing else. A human being is not a dog, a cat, a bird, a fish, a computer chip, or a stream of photons—"A is A" and man is man. Or as the philosopher/novelist Ayn Rand once stated, in terms of the sheerest, broadest fundamentals entailing awareness of identity and causality, "Man is a specific organism of a specific nature that requires specific actions to sustain his life."

Birth defects and genetic anomalies notwithstanding, the physical identity of the human species is characterized by the fact that each member's anatomy is comprised of organelles, cells, tissues, organs, and appendages whose physiologic principles of organization and function are common to all. Medical science—and bodybuilding science—is based on an understanding of the universality of the principles of human anatomy and physiology. This stems from the fact that reality is knowable, that its principles are discoverable by anyone possessing a rational and objective mind. As such, it cannot be the swirling, indeterminate flux that is put forth by many of the bodybuilding authorities. The fact that reality and its principles (i.e., the laws of physics) are immutable is what makes it possible for NASA to send men into space and bring them back safely each time. Likewise, if the principles of physiology didn't apply to everyone—if every individual's cells, organs, and muscles were constituted and functioned differently—medical science could not exist and doctors couldn't make diagnoses, perform surgeries, or dispense medicines.

While this last statement may seem redundant to some, considering the near-universal confusion concerning the fact that there is a valid theory of bodybuilding science, such tautology is necessary. It is precisely this fact that the principles of human anatomy and physiology are universal (i.e., applicable to all members of the species) that makes the sciences of medicine and bodybuilding viable intellectual disciplines. Any attempt to refute the validity of either of these theoretical sciences requires proof that some humans are not human, that they do not all possess the same fundamental defining characteristics. Since human beings are capable of rational thought and are also classified by science as an animal species (in fact, Aristotle defined the species man as the "rational animal"), one would have to marshal irrefutable evidence that there are human beings that exist who do not possess an animal's anatomy and physiology—or a rational faculty. A pretty tall order, indeed (I wouldn't hold my breath while looking for such a creature).

As pointed out in the last chapter, the pillars of bodybuilding orthodoxy are resting on a very shaky foundation. Their ideological base

"Anatomically and physiologically, every human being is essentially the same."—Mike Mentzer

consists of the notion that because we are all different, each individual bodybuilder requires a different training method. And, of course, in the most fundamental sense, each individual is different from every other in that each occupies a definite, different space in time. Also, psychologically, each is different in that every individual possesses the unique stamp of an unrepeatable mental character or personality. But more important in the context of medical/bodybuilding science is the fact that, anatomically and physiologically, every human being is essentially the same.

I emphasize the term *essentially* here because, while it is true that certain anatomical and physiologic features may vary among individuals, such variations exist within a limited measurable range, without altering the fact that the basic governing principles are the same, without altering the essence of man's animal aspect, his physical nature. For example, the fact that some humans don't possess the gastric enzymes necessary for digesting dairy products doesn't alter the fact that, nutritionally, each requires a well-balanced diet; that some people have lesser or greater melanin (skin pigment) doesn't alter the fact that all require the presence of sunlight to obtain a suntan; that some have higher IQs than others doesn't alter the fact that each must volitionally gain knowledge to think and survive; or the fact that there are endomorphs, ectomorphs, and mesomorphs doesn't alter the fundamental fact that each requires a high-intensity, anaerobic exercise stress to induce strength and muscular size increases. I will prove to you over the next few chapters that low to moderate aerobic training will not work better to develop the muscles than high-intensity, or anaerobic, exercise. And the reason it can't be done is that "A is A"—the principle of identity.

Recently, I was discussing the "one valid scientific theory of bodybuilding exercise" controversy with one of my in-the-gym training clients, the esteemed Dr. Gregory Kay, a highly trained Western theoretical medical scientist. An experienced cardiac surgeon with a close to 100 percent success rate in the surgical suite, and a man who performs more than 300 open-heart operations a year, Dr. Kay made the point, in effect, that his success, not to mention the overall success rate of modern medical science, is proof that there is and can be only one valid theory of medicine. To which I added, "That indirectly proves the same for bodybuilding science."

To stress the point one step further: if you were to find yourself by some quirk of fate back in the time of the Dark Ages, and you happened upon a member of the medical community of that era treating sickness with whatever knowledge he had at that point in time, he would have had close to a zero percent success rate with his patients. Then suppose you introduced him to the modern miracle of medical science, with its logical diagnostic procedure, antibiotics, analgesics, sterile technique, and surgery. If you survived being burned at the stake for possessing such magic powers, and if he adopted this theoretical approach to medicine, his medical success would skyrocket off the charts.

"Reality dictates how you must guide your training efforts to successfully develop larger muscles; and the nature of reason determines how you must guide your thinking so as to achieve intellectual independence."—Mike Mentzer

For bodybuilding authorities—"authorities," no less—to therefore say that all approaches have the same merit, is tantamount to stating that the intellectual method of the Dark Ages doctor is as likely to correct a brain aneurysm as would the intellectual method of a modern day neurosurgeon. Obviously, there is a life-and-death difference between the application of false ideas and the application of true ideas. Knowledge (truly valid ideas), after all, is our species' means of achieving all of its goals, including that final goal or end that makes the others possible—the maintenance of life itself.

THE IDENTITY OF THE HUMAN MIND

Speaking of intellectual method, just as there are valid principles to guide you successfully on your journey toward the acquisition of larger muscles, there is also a valid method, or theory, to guide one's thinking toward the acquisition of valid human knowledge. And it only stands to reason that a bodybuilder should want to know that the ideas (or principles) directing his training efforts are true ideas. And how will he ever come to distinguish true ideas from false ideas until or unless he learns something about the nature of ideas, which requires knowledge of the identity of the human mind. To settle for anything less than certainty about the truth of the ideas guiding you in the pursuit of your goals would be to leave your life literally to chance.

Remember that the identity of an entity determines how it will act: entities act only in accordance with their nature and cannot act otherwise. Just as the identity of man's physical character dictates that certain specific causes be enacted to effect the buildup of muscle tissue beyond normal levels, so the identity of man's mind dictates the specific intellectual causes that must be enacted to effect the acquisition of valid knowledge.

You Are the Ultimate Authority

All of the intellectual advances made by philosophy and science have resulted from man's use of reason and logic to identify the nature of that which exists. Your consciousness, like your body and all else that exists, has an identity; it is a faculty with a specific nature and that functions through specific means.

The so-called authorities I have alluded to depend for their power and authority on you relinquishing your consciousness in favor of theirs—but it's a control that only you can give

them. If you abdicate the responsibility of learning the nature of your own consciousness, your means of survival, then you can never control it: thus you unknowingly deliver yourself into the power of someone other than you—someone who might just have your worst interests at heart, whether he's trying to sell you a product you don't need, an erroneous training theory, or that theory of politics known as socialist dictatorship. Francis Bacon once said that, "Nature, to be commanded, must be obeyed." The nature (or identity) of reality dictates how you must guide your training efforts to successfully develop larger muscles, and the nature of reason determines how you must guide your thinking so as to achieve intellectual independence to determine for yourself what is true and certain.

The human mind is a rational faculty, which means that it has the capacity to reason, and reason is the faculty that identifies and integrates the material provided by your senses. Unlike the other animal species, which are guided automatically and unerringly by their instincts, humans are given nothing automatically. Everything a man or woman wants and needs, both existentially and spiritually—

Mentzer employed the faculty of reason to guide all of his training efforts.

whether food, shelter, clothing, big muscles or certainty, serenity, happiness, and a mature rational philosophy—requires that they volitionally choose to make the mental effort necessary to focus their perception and thought outward toward reality; only in this way can humans gain knowledge.

Knowledge, like the mind, also has an identity or nature, which is that it is hierarchical in structure. It has a foundation consisting of fundamental ideas and principles. On top of this base, human knowledge spirals upward in logical progression toward higher and more complex derivative concepts and principles. The hierarchical structure of human knowledge can be most readily observed in mathematics where the fundamentals are addition, subtraction, multiplication, and division. It is only on the basis of understanding these fundamentals that one may move logically, i.e., step by step, toward increasingly more complex derivative aspects of mathematics, such as algebra and calculus.

A human being's basic method of gaining knowledge is logic. Ayn Rand stated that:

> Man's means to establish the truth of his answers is logic, and logic rests on the axiom that existence exists. Logic is the art of non-contradictory identification. No concept man forms is valid unless he integrates it without contradiction into the total sum of his thinking. To arrive at a contradiction is to confess an error in one's thinking; to maintain a contradiction is to abdicate one's mind and to evict oneself from the realm of reality.

Aristotle (credited as the founder of logic) stated that the whole of logic is predicated on the Law of Non-Contradiction, that a thing is what it is and cannot be something else at the same time and in the same respect. In other words a muscle is a muscle—with its own distinct identity and qualities—it is not a mind, despite one popular bodybuilding "principle" of "muscle confusion." Given that the principle of identity applied to human muscle tissue reveals that it cannot reason or properly use

the principles of thought, one must wonder then how it might become confused.

Only the human mind, embracing the volitional responsibility of rational thought and critical judgment, that has chosen to learn the proper use of logic, can grasp principles and utilize them to formulate valid theories, design Apollo rockets, compose and conduct symphonies, extravasate a subdural hematoma, and create all the wonderful things that make our existence so different from that of any other living species.

A man's mind is a man's mind, and logic is logic. There is no such thing as "polylogic"; there is no "Aryan logic"; no "maternal logic"; no "minority logic"—there is only the logic of the human species and it is the art and skill of non-contradictory identification (and subsequent integration) of the material our senses perceive.

The reason behind the ongoing disintegration of bodybuilding and, indeed, most of the problems facing our culture these days is the belief of certain authorities and intellectuals that man's mind is somehow something divorced from logic or that logic is—somehow—a foreign or alien influence that obscures or distorts a human being's ability to discern and successfully interpret the facts of reality. In short, it is their attempt to excise human consciousness from the root of its very nature, its very identity. How many times have you heard certain bodybuilding authorities say the following: "It may be true for you, but it's not true for me." "Don't be so sure, nobody can be certain of anything." "It may be good in theory, but it doesn't work in practice." "It's logical, but logic has nothing to do with reality." While we've all heard them over and over, few realize their profound philosophic implications. They all say something about the nature of reality, human beings, and the efficacy of the human mind in gaining knowledge of reality, which, as we've seen, can be a matter of life and death.

These catch phrases amount to nothing more than a prescription for subjectivism. Their essential meaning is that reality is not discoverable by human knowledge; it is not an objective absolute, so therefore, universal principles cannot exist and the human mind, perforce, is powerless to discern them. It is a chasing of the wind. When someone says there is no such thing as a valid theory of anything, he is implying, in effect, that reality is not real, that "A is not A" and therefore no one can be certain of anything. An interesting position to hold, admittedly, if only for the fact that the statement is incompatible with its own content. It is self-contradictory because the statement itself is a theory. The same thing applies to the idea that no one can be certain—since it is being posited as a claim to truth, it also includes the speaker's confidence in his own position (since no one can be certain, he can't be certain that he can't be certain). In fact, such positions imply that their opposite is true—that certainty is possible and it is logic that points out the faults in such reasoning (logic actually refers to these as fallacies; specifically, the fallacy of self-exclusion or excluded middle).

Philosophically, those who claim knowledge is available without thought are referred to as mystics, while those who claim that knowledge is not possible are skeptics. Prior to my recently proclaiming that the theory of high-intensity training is the one and only valid theory of bodybuilding exercise, the implicitly held attitude of the bodybuilding authorities was mystic. Because no one till that time had ever fully focused on the issue of truth and falsehood, they all implicitly agreed to hand each other an intellectual/moral blank check; in effect, "Hey, I won't bring up the issue if you don't; then we can continue to pretend we're experts and make money. May the most ruthless win."

The mystic is someone who abdicates the effort and responsibility of the scrupulously exacting use of logic. It's as if he believes that by merely stating the arbitrary contents of his subconscious on a piece of paper, he has created a valid theory and should be accorded your respect. Since my proclamation, most of the mystics in bodybuilding have now become

Mentzer advocated high-intensity training because he saw for himself the reasons for its validity: that human muscle physiology has a specific nature that responds in a specific way to the stress of exercise.

skeptics, their position now being that there cannot be just one valid theory, or that nobody knows for certain what's true, or—more directly personal—"Who does Mentzer think he is! Who's to say what's right?"

In truth, my position has never been "Who's right?" but rather "What's true?" The theory of high-intensity exercise is not true because I say it's true. I discovered that it was true as a result of seeing for myself the evidence for its validity. And the lynchpin of this was learning that human muscle physiology has a specific nature and that it responds in a specific way to the stress of exercise. Which brings us to the identification of our second principle—that of intensity.

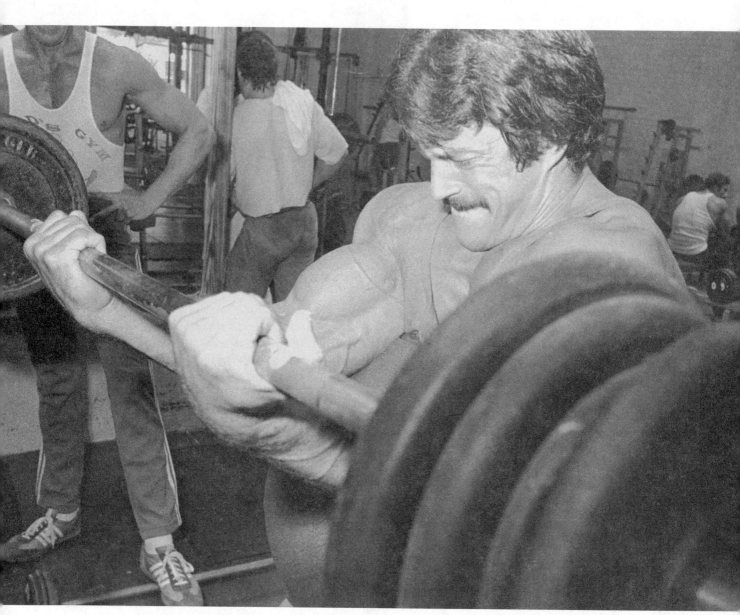

The stimulus required to induce the biochemical changes that result in muscle growth is high-intensity muscular contraction.

Chapter 5

THE SECOND PRINCIPLE
INTENSITY

We've seen that the first step toward an understanding of the science of bodybuilding begins with the recognition that while it's true that people differ in terms of personality and outer appearance, anatomically and physiologically we are all essentially the same. The second step logically follows from the first: the biochemical changes that result in muscle growth are the same in all individuals and the specific stimulus required to induce those biochemical changes is also the same. And it just so happens that this specific stimulus is high-intensity muscular contraction.

It is a readily observed fact that men and women who engage in highly repetitive tasks, such as laborers, distance runners, and swimmers, show little improvement in their muscular size or strength as a result of their efforts. Such tasks being by nature of low intensity, they do little to stimulate the body's musculature into inordinate levels of growth. It has been well documented for more than eight decades within the world of exercise physiology[1] that high-intensity muscular contraction is the most important requirement for the stimulation of rapid increases in muscular size and strength, whereas the duration of the exercise is not important in this regard. Moreover, high-intensity muscular contraction prevents even the possibility of a large number of such contractions within a given unit of time.

In terms of practical application to bodybuilding, this means that the harder a person trains, the less time he will be able to spend in

1. Research conducted by Roux-Lange indicated the following: "Only when a muscle performs with greatest power, i.e., through overcoming a greater resistance than before in a unit of time, will its functional cross-section need to increase. . . . Hypertrophy is seen only in muscles that must perform a great amount of work in a unit of time" (Lange, *Ueber Funktionelle Anpassung* USW, Berlin, Julius Springer, 1917). Further research by Petow and Siebert put a finer point on the intensity issue: "Hypertrophy results from an increase in the intensity of work done, whereas the total amount of work done is without significance" (W. Siebert and H. Petow, *Studien uber Arbeitshypertrophie des Muskels*, Z. Klin Medl, 102, 427–433, 1925). Research conducted by Arthur H. Steinhaus stated: "Only when intensity is increased does hypertrophy follow." (A. Steinhaus, *The Journal of the Association for Physical and Mental Rehabilitation*, Vol. 9. No. 5, Sep–Oct, 1955, 147–150).

"Attempting that last seemingly impossible rep causes the body to dip into its reserve ability."
—Mike Mentzer

such training. Intensity and duration, in other words, exist in an inverse ratio to one another; you can either train hard or you can train long, but you can't do both (recall Aristotle's law of Non-Contradiction—you see, there is already a logical integration of these various principles forming). And since we all want big muscles in the shortest time possible we must cut our training time back so that we are able to train as hard as is required to grow large muscles quickly.

Intensity, as applied to bodybuilding, can best be defined as the percentage of momentary ability that an individual is capable of exerting. The bodybuilder must regularly make the attempt to perform those tasks that seem impossible at the moment. Attempting that last seemingly impossible rep causes the body to dip into its reserve ability. Since the body has only relatively small quantities of reserve ability to draw upon before depletion and tissue loss occurs, the body will protect itself from

future assaults on its precious reserves by enlarging upon its normal ability through the compensatory buildup of more muscle mass.

Only high-intensity training can force the body to resort to its reserve ability sufficiently to stimulate compensatory growth. Repeating tasks that are already easy will do very little to stimulate growth. If, for example, you were to end a set just because an arbitrarily chosen number of reps have been completed or because the reps had begun to get difficult, very little growth stimulation will have been induced. With each succeeding rep of a set, your chances of stimulating growth increase because a greater percentage of your momentary ability will be required to continue. If a person is capable of pressing 150 pounds for a maximum of 10 reps, it is evident that the intensity of the first rep would be very low, since he has to exert only a very small percentage of his momentarily possible ability. As he fatigues with each succeeding rep, the situa-

"Carrying a set to a point where you are forced to utilize 100 percent of your momentary ability is the single most important factor in increasing size and strength."—Mike Mentzer

tion improves; he will then be required to exert an increasingly greater percentage of his momentary ability. The tenth, or last possible, rep will be of the highest intensity since an all-out effort requiring close to 100 percent of his momentary ability will be called upon.

Carrying a set to a point where you are forced to utilize 100 percent of your momentary ability is the single most important factor in increasing size and strength. Working to this "point of failure," when another rep is impossible despite the greatest effort, ensures that you pass through the "break-over point," a point in the set below which growth cannot be stimulated, and above which growth will be stimulated. Once you transcend this break-over point in the area of intensity, your results will increase geometrically. And for every degree over the break-over point, there will be—as there must be—a dramatic reduction in the amount of time you spend training at that intensity level.

INCREASING THE INTENSITY LEVEL

Anything that you do to make your workout harder will be a step in the right direction. Raising the intensity factor in your workouts can be done in three ways:

1. By progressively increasing the amount of weight you use.
2. By progressively decreasing the amount of time it requires to perform a certain amount of work.
3. By carrying each set to a point of total failure.

Every time we witness an increase in our strength, the amount of weight used must be increased. If you can presently curl 100 pounds for a maximum of six reps, and one week from now your strength increases and allows you 10 reps in the curl with 100 pounds, the weight should be increased by as much as is required

Mike Mentzer performs a high-intensity set of leg extensions.

to lower your maximum rep performance to six again. Such is the true nature of progressive resistance weight training.

Decreasing the amount of time it takes to perform a certain task is a relatively simple matter. An unceasing effort must be made to decrease the amount of time required to complete a given workout. If your current workout takes you two hours to complete, then completing it in one hour would double the intensity, and thus the effectiveness, of your workouts. Doing the same workout in less time is often only a matter of motivation and intent. Do not, however, increase the speed of your workout in order to beat the clock. If you move too quickly from one exercise to another, you may become light-headed or nauseous. If at

first you require a few minutes rest between sets, don't fret. Over a period of time you'll adapt to the increased stress levels, which should enable you to reduce the rest period between sets. Rushing too fast at first will only reduce your efficiency; and you won't be able to train with the intense effort required to stimulate muscular growth. Take it easy at first and your workout time will eventually decrease.

The third variable in raising the intensity factor—training to total failure—may be somewhat vague, and will require a more elaborate explanation. What does training to failure mean? To continue doing a set until you can't perform even a partial movement? Or does it mean to terminate a set when a complete rep is no longer possible? Could it possibly mean that you should continue to perform set after endless set until you are so exhausted you are forced to end the workout?

THE THREE LEVELS OF SKELETAL MUSCLE STRENGTH

The skeletal muscles all have three levels of strength. The first, and weakest, level of strength is the muscle's ability to raise a weight from a position of full extension to one of full contraction. This is also known as positive strength, or concentric contraction. The second level of strength is static and it refers to the fact that the same muscle is stronger in a position of stasis, i.e., it can hold more weight at any one point in that muscle's range of motion than the muscle can raise in a positive manner. For example, if an individual could curl a maximum weight of 125 pounds for one rep, he should be able to hold approximately 150 pounds or more at any given point in the range of motion of a curl for several seconds. The third and remaining level of strength is the strongest, and that is the lowering of a weight under control, from the fully contracted to the fully extended position. This controlled lowering of a weight is also known as negative resistance or eccentric contraction. The individual who is capable of curling 125 pounds for a maximum of one rep, and of holding 150

A muscle has three levels of strength: positive (raising), static (holding), and negative (lowering). All three levels must be trained in order to stimulate maximum muscle growth.

You can only be said to have trained with maximum intensity when you have exerted 100 percent of your momentary ability.

pounds in a static position somewhere in the range of motion of a curl would have the ability to lower 175 pounds or even 200 pounds in the curl.

Considering, then, that a muscle has three levels of strength, it is obvious that you must exhaust all three levels before a state of total muscular failure can be reached. If a person who can press 150 pounds for a maximum of 10 reps terminates the set upon conclusion of the tenth positive rep, he cannot be said to have trained to total muscular failure since he still has a generous measure of both his static and negative levels of strength available. Nor can he be said to have trained with maximum intensity since he hasn't exerted 100 percent of his momentary ability. Only if he were to continue the set, after the last positive rep, by the continued lowering of the weight under control to a point of failure, will he reach a point of total muscular failure and thus have exerted maximum intensity of effort.

The fact that many bodybuilders have built outstanding physiques with low-intensity marathon workouts of the daily three-hour-per-session variety proves nothing; they would have developed farther and faster, or reached their present level sooner, had they trained properly with high-intensity training. And anyone who trains six days a week for hours each day, and then says he is training hard, doesn't know what hard training is. He may be training diligently for long periods, but he isn't training hard. High-intensity training is brutally hard, which is the very reason it cannot be carried on for prolonged periods of time. Until you either experience it for yourself or watch someone else do it, you can't possibly appreciate it.

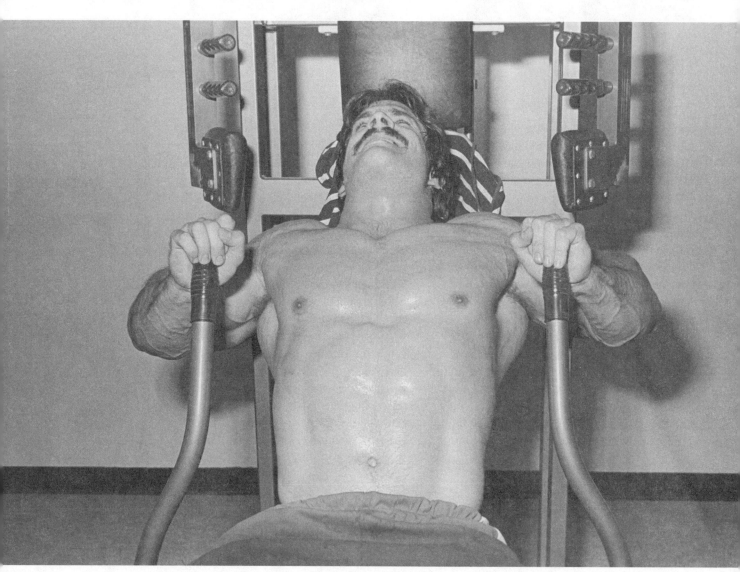

"Any exercise carried on beyond the least amount required to stimulate an optimal increase is not merely a waste of effort, it is actually highly counterproductive."—Mike Mentzer

Chapter 6

THE THIRD PRINCIPLE
DURATION

Once you've grasped the fact that high intensity of effort (training to failure) is the sole factor responsible for growth stimulation, the logical question that arises is how many such sets should be performed? It is precisely on this point that most weight trainers make their gravest error. Any exercise carried on beyond the least amount required to stimulate an optimal increase is not merely a waste of effort, it is actually highly counterproductive.

The fact that recovery ability is strictly limited leads ineluctably to a logically warranted conclusion: the issue of duration, or the volume of sets, whether 1 set or 100 sets is performed, is a negative factor—negative with a capital N. In other words, the extent to which you work out (perform a number of sets) is a negative because for every set performed there is caused a deeper inroad into recovery ability; this is undeniably a negative factor. For every set performed, more and more of the body's limited reserve of biochemical resources is used in the attempt to merely recover from, or compensate for, the exhaustive effects of the work-

out, leaving that much less left over for overcompensation in the form of new muscle.

So, clearly the issue of volume is a negative factor. Even one set is a negative; insofar that you train at all you are utilizing biochemical resources that must be replaced, and the more you use the more that must be replaced. It follows logically that optimal results can be achieved only as the result of the least, or precise, amount of exercise necessary being performed. Of course, at least one set must be performed to have a workout. As training must be of a very high intensity in order to stimulate muscle growth, and as the higher the intensity, the lower the duration of the workout, a high-intensity workout must, by its very nature (again, the principle of identity) be very brief.

With a truly scientific, theoretical approach to exercise, there is no room for the traditional or the arbitrary. So the proper attitude is to go into the gym like a rational human being and perform only the precise amount of exercise required by nature. More is not better; less is not better; the precise amount

As Mentzer often pointed out, "The intensity/duration ratio is inverse; you can train hard or you can train long, but you can't do both—and it just so happens that it takes hard training to build big muscles." Mentzer hits it hard on the Nautilus triceps extension machine.

required is best. And as it turns out, the precise amount of exercise required by nature is less than anyone realized until recently.

Up to a very definite point, imposing a high-intensity-training stress on your body will result in an adaptive, compensatory development of muscle tissue—but performing one set beyond the least amount required will make unnecessary inroads into your recovery ability and hamper the process of growth production. Carried to extremes—as with the marathon six-day-a-week variety of training—the body's recuperative subsystems will no longer be able to compensate for the exhaustive effects of the exercise session, and a state of decompensation (depletion and tissue loss) will occur.

THE ECONOMICS OF GROWTH AND RECOVERY

Energy is the most precious thing in the universe; without it the planets would cease to revolve, the sun would cool off, and life could no longer exist. It is the first requisite from which everything else follows. Bodybuilders needn't be reminded of the central importance of energy since plenty of readily available energy is needed for the brutally hard workouts required to stimulate large-scale increases in size and strength.

Our physical bodies, like the planet earth, possess only limited resources—a finite energy supply. The energy our bodies utilize is derived from the sun, the food we eat, and the air we breathe. It is absolutely essential, of course, that we continue to consume sufficient quantities of calories and nutrients because we all have only a limited reserve of fuel, and we would thus eventually die if we failed to replace what we continually use up.

The acquisition and preservation of energy is the principal concern of all living creatures. Energy is needed to find food, to fend off our enemies, and to reproduce. As bodybuilders we require extra energy to fuel our grueling workouts and also to grow on. Many bodybuilders

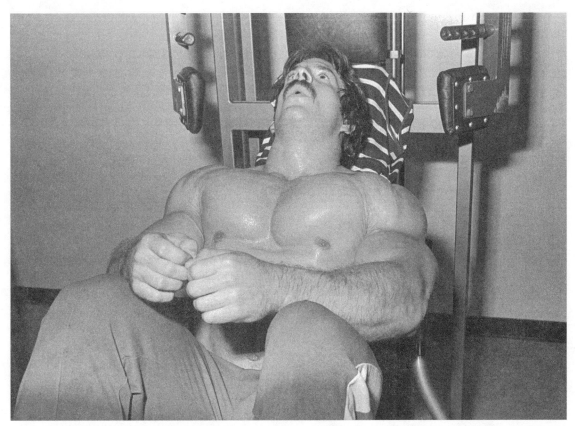

The first thing the body must do following a high-intensity workout is recover the energy that was used up during the workout—this can take upwards of one week to accomplish.

overlook the very important fact that energy is required for growth. Growth—at least growth that transcends normal levels—is a very minor concern to the body. While it is self-evident that sufficient energy is required to carry on those activities that enable us to survive, few would argue the fact that a 20-inch arm or a Mr. Universe physique does little to enhance survival.

The first thing our bodies must attempt to do following a workout is to recover the energy it lost as a result of the workout. When we train too long and do not allow enough time for recuperation, the body will fail to recover the energy and physical resources it expended during the workout. When too much of our energy is spent actually training, as with the six-day-a-week, 20-sets-per-bodypart variety, then all of the body's resources are wasted in the attempt to overcome the purely exhaustive effects of the workout, with nothing left over for growth.

HOW THE BODY COPES WITH STRESS

The principle of duration might be made clearer if we looked at it in terms of the body's capacity to cope with stress. While we are exposed to multitudinous forms of stress every day of our lives, there are three forms of physical stress we bodybuilders can all identify with: the stress of the sun on the skin, the stress of abrasive friction to the palms of our hands, and the stress of exercise on our muscles. In addition to the localized effect of stress—to the skin, the palms, and the muscles—there exists a generalized effect on the body's entire system, or systemic stress.

Up to a very definite point, exposure to the sun will lead to the formation of a tan. Once we exceed that rather definite point, however, and overexpose the skin, blisters will form instead of a tan. Carried to radical extremes, overexposure to the sun's rays will cause stroke, poisoning, and even death. Having exceeded the threshold point, the body's recuperative subsystems will no longer be able to successfully cope with the stress of the sun, and the skin will begin to break down and burn.

The formation of the tan is the result of a compensatory process of the body designed to allow us to cope more successfully with the same stress in the near future, and with less disturbance of the body's resources. The blisters and the burn are examples of a reverse process of depletion: instead of building up the protective tissue (tan), the body decompensated and lost tissue (burn). The buildup of a callus on the palm of one's hand is much the same. The skin on the palms of our hands is generally much thicker than the rest of our skin, as protection from constant contact with rough abrasive objects. The handling of extremely rough objects, like the knurled barbell grip, subjects the skin on our palms to intense stress through friction, and often causes the already tough hide on the palms to break down. If friction is abrasive enough, the formation of a callus will be stimulated. Then, if the amount of friction was insufficient to wear away the growth of the callus as it was forming, a callus would indeed form. While the friction had to be intense and abrasive enough to stimulate the formation of a callus, too much would cause blisters and the wearing away of the skin completely.

Here again, as with the stress of the sun, the stress of abrasive friction applied to the palms of the hands will result in a compensatory buildup of extra skin that will prevent the wearing away of the skin when exposed to similar stress (friction) in the near future. Carried to extremes, however, the body won't be able to build up the callus rapidly enough to compensate for the demands placed on it, and a reverse process of depletion will occur, caus-

ing blisters and an eventual tearing away of the skin altogether.

Barbell training can be examined in much the same light as was exposure of the skin and abrasive friction on the palms. Exercise is a form of stress to the muscles and the overall physical system. Intense exercise will stimulate a compensatory buildup of added muscle tissue, which will enable the body to cope with the stress of intense exercise again in the near future with less disturbance and fewer demands on the body's limited resources. Taken to extremes, as is the case with most bodybuilders who overtrain, the exercise will place a drain on the recuperative subsystems of the body that prevents the buildup of added muscle tissue because all of the reserves will be used up in an attempt to overcome the depletion caused by the overtraining. Keep in mind the primacy of energy; added tissue growth is a minor concern when compared to the acquisition and recovery of our precious physical energy.

These facts strongly suggest that the less time spent in the gym actually training, the better. Once you have stimulated growth, with the required high-intensity training, *get out of the gym!* Even if you are unwilling, or simply unable, to train with the intensity required to stimulate rapid large-scale increases in size and strength, don't make the mistake of thinking you will make up for the lack of training intensity by performing added low-intensity sets. After all, you are still better off doing two or three sets improperly than you are doing four, five, ten, or any greater number of sets improperly. The additional sets are not just wasted; they are highly counterproductive in that they place an unnecessary drain on your body's resources that might otherwise have been used in the process of overcompensation and growth.

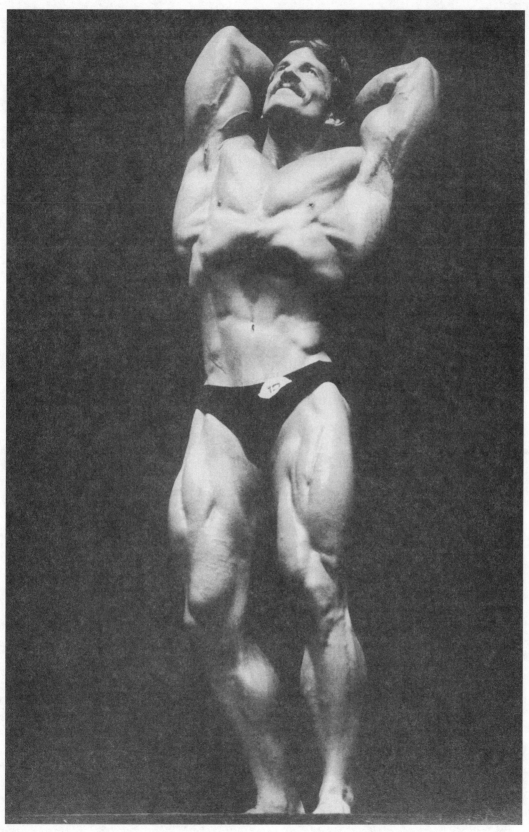

If your workouts aren't too long in duration, your recovery process should be fully completed prior to your next workout. This will allow your muscles to become stronger and your ability to generate more intense contractions will increase proportionately.

Mike Mentzer
heads to the gym
for a workout
after first having
allowed his mus-
cles and recupera-
tive subsystems
ample time for
recovery and
growth.

Chapter 7

THE FOURTH PRINCIPLE
FREQUENCY

Let us consider the principle of frequency. Many top bodybuilders train six days a week for up to several hours a day. We should know by now that it does not necessarily follow that such training methods were directly responsible for their development. Top bodybuilders all possess metabolisms that give them a higher tolerance to the stress of exercise: because of a hereditary advantage, they can cope more successfully with high levels of stress than can the average person. Had they trained for shorter periods with high-intensity methods, many of these top bodybuilders could have developed further or might have reached their current levels of development much sooner.

The amount of stress that the body can successfully cope with and that will cause a buildup effect somewhere in the body is directly related to the intensity of the stress. While the degree of stress must be intense enough to stimulate a compensatory buildup (because no amount of a stress that is below the required intensity level will produce the desired result), a very small amount of high-intensity stress is required to produce the buildup of new tissue; and the greater the intensity, the less the body will tolerate before decompensating and heading the other way into a state of depletion and tissue loss.

Having stressed the body sufficiently with high-intensity training, you must then leave the body alone and not exercise it further, thus allowing time for it to respond with a compensatory buildup of new tissue. While the stimulation of added growth will occur almost immediately, the actual growth cannot take place immediately. Adequate rest is needed.

Many bodybuilders wrongly believe that a split routine of six days a week, with one-half of the muscles exercised on one day and then rested on the following day while the other half are being exercised, will provide the rest required for adequate growth following exercise. You must remember that exercise always has a generalized effect on the entire physical system as well as a localized one on specific muscles. So, even though you may be affording your alternately worked muscles a certain

It is not just your muscles that need time to recover but also your entire physical system, which is why training every day is always a mistake.

amount of rest on a six-day split routine, you are not providing the needed rest for the overall physical system when you tax it with every-day training.

The tendency among enthusiastic bodybuilders is to add more sets to their workouts, as well as to increase the number of days a week they train. This tendency must be kept in check and avoided at all costs. As a bodybuilder begins to grow larger and stronger as a result of proper training, the likelihood of overtraining looms ever greater because as the body grows stronger its ability to generate intensity increases, which, you must keep in mind, places greater stress on the body and

thus calls for less training. The majority of bodybuilders do just the opposite: as they progress, they add to the amount, which will slow down their progress. This leads to desperation and more irrational thinking.

It is at this point that many will add even more to their workouts, causing an even greater decrease in progress and more desperation. It is a never-ending cycle. From the time a beginner starts training, she has the potential to increase her strength some 300 percent, while her capacity to tolerate exercise or recover from the stress of exercise only improves by 50 percent. As you progress, every effort must be made to increase the intensity of your workout, which

"It is the body that produces growth—but only if left undisturbed during a sufficient rest period."
—Mike Mentzer

will then lead to a corresponding decrease in the amount of time you can engage in such training.

The vast majority of bodybuilding trainees sell themselves short. Erroneously attributing their lack of satisfactory progress to a poverty of genetic traits (instead of their irrational and counterproductive training practices), they give up training. Don't make the same mistake. Don't believe that all training systems and the-

ories are of equal validity and then waste precious years of your life frantically trying one after the other.

Just as there is only one reality, one set of universal objective principles governing the physiological activities of the human body, so there can be only one valid theory, one set of abstract principles, of productive exercise.

In order for a training routine or workout to be productive it must, of course, stimulate

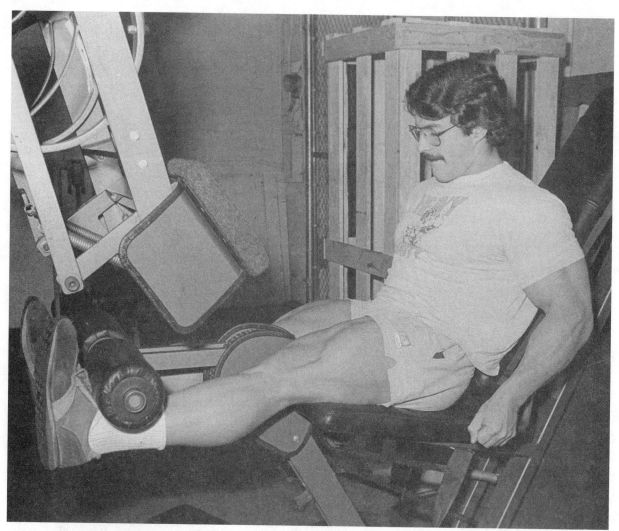

The workout stimulates growth but it does not allow that growth to manifest—growth is produced during your time away from the gym, when you are resting and recovering.

growth. However, a workout that stimulates growth must also allow growth to be produced (again, please note the distinction between growth stimulation and growth production). This means that the routine must not be carried on so long or repeated so frequently that it depletes the body's reserves in an attempt to compensate for the merely exhaustive effects of the workout with nothing leftover for over-compensation, i.e., growth production. An ideal workout, then, should induce maximum growth stimulation and utilize a minimum of the body's biochemical reserves. With a properly conducted high-intensity training program, these two requirements of an ideal routine can be fulfilled.

We know by now that high-intensity effort is an absolute requirement for stimulating rapid increases in strength and size, and that since high-intensity training must be of short duration, it will deplete relatively little of the body's reserves. By definition, overtraining means performing any more exercise, in terms of both duration and frequency, than is precisely required.

Most bodybuilders today apparently don't understand that the big picture essentially involves two elements of equal value; literally 50–50, not 70–30 or 60–40, but 50–50, with neither of the two elements being slightly more important than the other. The first element is the workout itself, of course; the second ele-

Once you've stimulated growth through your efforts in the gym, it is time to leave the gym—and grow!

ment is the rest period between workouts. The workout, understand, doesn't produce muscle growth, but merely serves to stimulate the body's growth mechanism into motion. It is the body that produces growth, but only if left undisturbed during a sufficient rest period.

Now here's the crux of the problem: how can one know with reasonable certainty just how much time needs to elapse between workouts? The answer is to be found in the following. Immediately upon completion of a workout, you don't feel the same as you did

immediately before the workout. Instead, you are exhausted. In addition to the subjective, or personal, experience of feeling fatigued, you are also exhausted, in the technical sense, in that a considerable portion of your body's limited reserve of biochemical resources, known as recovery ability, was used to fuel the workout. To the extent that one works out, in other words, performs a number of sets, he makes an inroad to his recovery ability. Visualize an inroad as a hole being dug into your reserves. You perform one set; a small hole is made. You perform a second set, a deeper hole; a third set, the hole is deeper still, and so forth.

The first thing your body must do after the workout is not build a mountain, i.e., the new muscle growth on top, but fill the hole you've made below. That is, it must recover, overcome the deficit, compensate for the exhaustive effects of the workout. Now the important point: the process of recovery is not completed in five minutes after the workout. In fact, the completion of the recovery process may take up to several days, probably even longer, before the body will have the opportunity to start building the mountain; i.e., produce muscle growth (keep in mind that if you work out again before the recovery process is completed, you will short-circuit the growth process).

That's right, the recovery process alone may take several days to be completed. And here's the proof. Every bodybuilder has had the experience of doing a tremendous leg workout, for instance, on a Friday afternoon, and then after resting all weekend, he wakes up Monday morning still tired. The fact that you're still fatigued on Monday—as a result of your Friday workout—is proof that you hadn't fully recovered even after 72 hours had elapsed. There is still a deficit; you still haven't filled that energy hole. And to work out that day would be a grave mistake. Because you're still in a hole, you would be disinclined to work out at all, and you'd be weaker than you were last workout. And to further disturb the physiology at this juncture with more exercise, you'd prevent the body from starting to build the mountain on top, the muscle—and you'd just start the digging of a deeper hole. Every bodybuilder has had the experience of being weaker one workout to the next. And this explains why.

Let's assume that, for some reason, you were forced to miss your scheduled workout on Monday, thus leaving the physiology undisturbed and affording your body the further opportunity it absolutely requires to fully compensate for the exhaustive effects of Friday's workout. When you wake up on Tuesday, you're no longer fatigued—not teeming with energy, mind you, but feeling recovered. Were you to go into the gym on Tuesday, having provided the body with the added opportunity it required to fully recover, your desire to train wouldn't be great, and you'd only be as strong as you were the last workout—no weaker, but no stronger either, only the same. And to work out at this point would again be a mistake because stressing the body with more exercise, you'd short-circuit the process of growth production just as it was about to begin.

Now let's assume you were forced to forego Tuesday's workout. And you wake up on Wednesday not just feeling recovered, but energetic and eager to train. In the gym you'd most likely be delighted as you'd be up 10 pounds on some exercises, a rep or two on others, and generally things would go well. Unbeknownst to you, however, as you hadn't yet read this book, it would be a mistake to train on Wednesday. Why? Because at that point the body only had the opportunity it required to fully recover, but it had produced something less than 100 percent of the mountain, or muscle. Had you waited one more day, your body would more likely have fully completed the growth production process, and you would have been up 20 or more pounds on some exercises and four or five reps on others.

Once I understood the above, the principle of frequency, I immediately switched my personal training clients from training every 48 to 72 hours to training every 96 to 120 hours—and the improvement in their progress has been absolutely phenomenal!

If you balance your intensity, duration, and frequency correctly, you will be a happy and successful bodybuilder.

The principle of specificity states that a certain type of training effort yields a certain type of training effect. In other words, if you want to train to build bigger muscles, you must train harder—not longer.

Chapter 8

THE FIFTH PRINCIPLE
SPECIFICITY

A corollary of the principles of identity and intensity is the principle of specificity. You will recall that the principle of identity states that everything which exists has an identity, that a thing is what it is and can be nothing else and that the principle of identity put into action affects the Law of Causality, or cause-and-effect, which states that an entity can act only in accord with its nature and cannot act otherwise.

To this end, for the development of the capacities of both muscular size/strength and cardiovascular endurance, specific forms of exercise must be employed. The fact that specific demands imposed upon the body result in specific neuro-physiological adjustments to those demands has been known for years by exercise physiologists. The term used to describe this well-authenticated scientific fact is *specificity*.

In addition to the demand having to be of a specific nature (principle one: identity), it must also be stressful enough to induce large-scale and rapid rates of improvement (principle

Training with submaximal weights and low intensity will be easy—and unproductive.

Training with maximal weights and high intensity will be difficult—and highly productive.

two: intensity). As a rule of thumb, the level of stress must exceed 50 percent of the individual's existing capacity. The more the stress exceeds the 50 percent level, the greater the rate of improvement. Therefore, if you wish to achieve the greatest and most rapid improvement that your genetically predetermined capacity will allow, you must exercise at the 100 percent level of your existing functional capacity.

It has been noted by experts that somewhere within the overall physical system a regulatory and sensory mechanism exists that regulates muscle growth. Once an individual matures to a point of normal or average adult muscular size and strength, the sensory part of the mechanism signals the growth-stimulating

portion to stop any further growth, as more is not needed for normal everyday living. As long as our activity remains within normal limits, our muscular size/strength levels will remain essentially unchanged, along with our percentage of reserve ability. In order to trigger the regulatory system into another growth cycle—growth that transcends normal adult levels of size and strength—the level of our activity must be raised above normal.

Remember that to induce specific physiologic changes—additional muscle growth in this case—specific demands must be imposed. The specific demand required to effect the fastest possible increases in muscular size and strength is directly related to the intensity of muscular contraction. The functional capacity

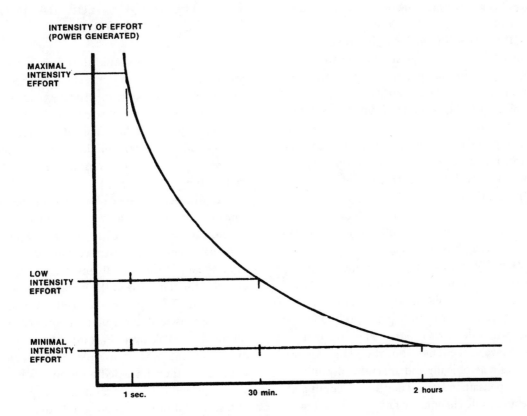

INTENSITY OF EFFORT
(POWER GENERATED)

MAXIMAL
INTENSITY
EFFORT

LOW
INTENSITY
EFFORT

MINIMAL
INTENSITY
EFFORT

1 sec.   30 min.   2 hours

The above graph demonstrates the relationship between fatigue (endurance time) and the power intensity generated during a workout. The greater the power intensity—the most important factor for inducing growth stimulation—the less the endurance. You can see on the graph that the point just above the one-second mark on the horizontal scale graphs out at maximal effort on the vertical scale. At two hours it graphs out at a very low intensity. If you sprint as fast as possible, you can only do it for a very short time, while if you jog you can keep it up for a much longer duration. If you train as hard as possible within each set, the fewer sets you will be able to do before fatigue obliterates you.

I am speaking of here is muscular contraction, and the closer we come to performing at a level where we cause a muscle to contract up to 100 percent, the greater the possibility of inducing a size/strength increase.

THE RELATIONSHIP OF EFFORT AND TIME

The reason for the lack of success of many bodybuilders is a confusion that has led them to a type of training that results more in an improvement of their cardiovascular system than in building muscle. Those who tend to

train often and for long periods—as with the six-day-a-week, two-hour-per-day routine—are imposing the wrong type of stress on their bodies for the stimulation of muscle growth. The fact that they are training for long periods precludes even the possibility of high-intensity muscular contraction. The graph above, which I created for one of my seminars, demonstrates the relationship between intensity of effort and the time element. This graph shows that an inverse ratio exists between the intensity of one's effort and the amount of time in which one is capable of engaging in an activity at a particular level of intensity. You'll note that for every increase in intensity there is, as there must be, a corresponding decrease in the time element.

If your specific goal is to improve your ability to carry out large volumes of work, then you must train in a specific fashion: aerobically, with low to moderate intensity, frequently employing a large volume of sets. If your specific goal is to increase your muscular size and strength, then you must also train in a specific manner: anaerobically, with high intensity, doing a low volume of sets relatively infrequently.

It's not as if the body has 100 units of resources available for adaptation in the form of size/strength increases and another 100 units available for adapting with increased endurance. There are only 100 units of adaptive energy available, period! Dividing these units between bodybuilding and endurance results in little or no progress in either area.

As we've seen, most bodybuilders grossly overtrain aerobically and anaerobically and decompensate in both. They lose strength and size and grow chronically fatigued. Training guided by mixed premises will not yield results of the same magnitude as adaptive-specific training. What this means in practical terms for the bodybuilder is that in order to train at the intensity level required to induce rapid increases in muscle growth, he cannot train for long periods.

Oh sure, anyone can train at high-intensity levels for short periods and then drastically reduce the intensity level and continue training at a lower level. The problem here is that low intensity of effort doesn't induce muscular growth but it does place a drain on our precious reserves, which could lead to a slowdown in progress. In cases of gross overtraining at low intensity, an actual regression of capacity occurs.

If your reason for training is to bring about the largest and most rapid increases in size and strength possible for your genetic potential, then you must train in such a fashion that the highest possible percentage of the muscular mass is involved. How does one go about ensuring that he will cause his muscles to contract maximally in an exercise? Certain factors are required to produce this situation.

FOUR TECHNIQUES FOR MAXIMUM MUSCLE STIMULATION

1. All exercises should start from a pre-stretched position. For a muscle to contract maximally it *must* start in a fully extended position in which the muscle actually involved is being mildly stretched. This pre-stretching sets up a neurological stimulus, known as the *myotatic reflex*, that allows for maximum contraction.

2. The performance of all of your exercises must be conducted at a relatively slow rate of speed. Exercises that are initiated with a sudden jerk or thrust, and then continued to the contracted position rapidly involve very little actual muscular mass in the completion of the movement. Once the speed exceeds a certain rate, the muscle slackens and the force of momentum takes over. Start all of your exercises deliberately, with no sudden thrust, and continue to the contracted position in a likewise slow and deliberate fashion. This practice will save a lot of wear and tear on your connective tissue as well as increase muscle involvement in your routines.

3. The range of movement of your exercise should be as great as possible. Since our muscles contract by producing movement, they must have the fullest possible range of movement if they are to contract fully. When I speak of full range of movement, I am referring to movement that causes a muscle to work against a resistance from a position of full extension to full contraction.

4. The resistance imposed upon the muscle must be sufficient to require it to contract maximally. The all-or-nothing principle of muscular function states that individual muscle fibers are incapable of performing varying degrees of work; they are either working as hard as possible or not at all. Performing a light movement does not require the slight involvement of the entire muscle; rather, only the exact number of fibers needed to perform that movement will be involved, but they will be contracting to the limit of their momentary ability. It follows then that to involve the entire bulk of a muscle in a movement, a load must be imposed that requires all of the fibers of

The position of pre-stretch (in exercises such as Preacher curls) triggers the myotatic reflex, which allows for maximal contraction to take place.

Mike Mentzer on the Nautilus leg extension machine puts his quadriceps muscles into the position of full contraction.

"To involve the bulk of a muscle in a movement, a load must be imposed that requires all of the fibers of that muscle to contract." Mentzer subjects Aaron Baker's muscles to just such a load while spotting him on a set of incline presses.

that muscle to contract. Since a muscle must be in its shortest, or fully contracted, position to involve all of its fiber in a contraction, sufficient resistance must be provided in the contracted position. Of course in many conventional exercises, like the barbell curl, there is no resistance at all in the contracted position, making it impossible to induce maximum growth stimulation with such exercises. A little thought and improvisation will lead you to exercises that provide resistance in the contracted position.

Exercises like concentration curls provide resistance in the peak, or fully contracted, position for greater muscle growth stimulation.

The summit and purpose of high-intensity training is to elicit an adaptive response from the body.

Chapter 9

THE SIXTH PRINCIPLE
ADAPTATION

Building muscle is the adaptation of the body to the stress of high-intensity exercise (providing, as we've seen in the previous two principles of duration and frequency, that the stress is provided in brief and infrequent dosages). This being the case, the crucible of muscle building is adaptation. In fact, all of the previous principles lead up to this principle; if human muscle (identity) only grows larger and stronger through the application of the proper training protocol (specificity) of high-intensity training (intensity), and such training in order to be of a high-intensity nature cannot be endured for long (duration) or engaged in very often (frequency), it will lead to the body adjusting itself to the stress of the imposed training stress by a process of adaptation (adaptation) by enlarging upon its existing store of muscle mass.

You can see that all of the principles thus far elucidated are integrated and that no one principle can do the trick in isolation from the other principles. But you should also see that the summit and purpose of high-intensity training is to elicit an adaptive response from

the body to the stress of high-intensity training. To this end, it is important to revisit principle one (identity) briefly so that we can learn the nature of stress and of adaptation, and how stress can be manipulated to trigger the body's adaptive mechanism.

Before moving to California to pursue a career as a professional bodybuilder, I lived in a suburb of Washington, D.C., and worked for a time as an assistant to Dr. John Ziegler.

Ziegler was something of a pioneer in sports medicine; he had been the physician for the American Olympic weightlifting team, had trained champion weightlifters and bodybuilders such as Bill March and Vern Weaver, and even had a hand in helping to develop the anabolic steroid Dianabol. Ziegler, in fact, is often cited as the person responsible for introducing anabolic steroids to the American sports scene—something I'm sure he considered a rather dubious distinction.

What made Dr. Ziegler even more interesting was his world-famous "electronic muscle stimulator." With the assistance of an electronics engineer, Ziegler developed a machine that could contract any of the body's skeletal muscles to varying degrees—including maximal contraction where every fiber of a given muscle is activated. The Federal Trade Commission investigated Ziegler's machine and claimed it was harmless because it supposedly didn't work. Well, the machine most certainly did work; my brother and I were giving each other treatments, as well as administering them to injured athletes and those who were handicapped or had lost the use of certain limbs.

My point in enumerating Ziegler's accomplishments—and actually these are but a few; he was accomplished in many areas—is to show that he was widely experienced in the field of exercise and therefore was a man from whom one could learn a great deal—and I did. The Doctor loved to talk to anyone who was willing to listen (as my brother and I always were) on just about any subject. He could discourse on any culture, past or present, for hours, describing their mores, their eating habits, or their mating rituals. Often he would regale us with stories about his travels with the American weightlifting team, all the time peppering his talk with the funniest anecdotes imaginable. When the subject got around to training—as it always would—he would invariably refer to a Dr. Hans Selye and how this man's research was responsible for shaping his own views on training and use of the electronic muscle stimulator. Ziegler never got specific as to who this Dr. Selye was or how he came to influence him, but he never failed to bring up the name.

It was some time later, after I had ceased working for the Doctor because of his failing health, that I was browsing through a bookstore—long one of my favorite pastimes. I happened upon a book entitled *The Stress of Life* whose author was, you guessed it, Hans Selye, M.D. The name had stuck in my mind, and I purchased the book immediately.

While Selye's book did not deal with weight training specifically, it was easy to see how someone could take his ideas and apply them to weight training. My own views regarding training and the principles of intensity and duration fit in nicely with what Selye had to say, but even more importantly his book gave me many new facts and concepts that I could incorporate into my training.

STRESS AND THE GENERAL ADAPTATION SYNDROME (G.A.S.)

Stress is a popular topic these days. We read about it in countless magazine articles; it's the favorite conversation point at cocktail parties. Since stress is talked about so often in so many different circles, it's bound to be misrepresented and misunderstood. For a precise definition of stress, I quote from Selye's book *The Stress of Life*: "Stress is the common denominator of all adaptive reactions in the body."

Further on, Selye gets more precise: "Stress is the state manifested by a specific syndrome which consists of all the nonspecifically induced changes within a biologic system."

In other words, stress has specific characteristics and composition but no particular cause. The human body is exposed to myriad stressors (stress-producing agents) day in and day out. These include pain, cold and hot weather, emotional stimuli, viral infections, and muscular activity, just to mention a few. While any number or combination of these things can induce a state of stress—thus making the cause nonspecific—the way that stress is manifested is always very specific.

Selye called the body's specific reaction to stress the *general adaptation syndrome*, or G.A.S. The G.A.S. consists of three distinct stages:

1. A general alarm reaction
2. A stage of resistance
3. A stage of exhaustion (if the stress persists)

Stress is present during all three of these stages, but its symptoms change. Most of the stressors that act upon us result in changes corresponding to the first and second stages of the G.A.S. At first the stresses alarm us—and then we get used to them. Only very severe stress leads to exhaustion and, if prolonged, death.

No matter what form the stress takes, the body's response to stress is always the same. This response is called the General Adaptation Syndrome.

In his book Selye applies the G.A.S. to the physical activity of running, pointing out that running produces a stress situation mainly in our muscles and the cardiovascular system. We cope with this first by limbering up and getting the organs ready for the task. Then we run at the height of efficiency for a while, but eventually exhaustion results. The limbering up and initial discomfort corresponds to the alarm stage, running efficiently is the stage of resistance and, of course, exhaustion is the third stage of the G.A.S. Dr. Selye goes on to illustrate how we go through the same three stages in other activities, and he concludes by saying: "Most human activities go through these three stages: we first have to get in the swing of things, then we get pretty good at them, but finally we tire of them."

The Nature of Adaptation

In the late 1800s, the noted French physiologist Claude Bernard stated that a characteristic of all living beings is their ability to keep their internal environment constant despite changes in the outside environment. The physical and chemical properties of our bodies remain incredibly constant in spite of the changes that always surround us. A person exposed to great heat or cold, for instance, doesn't experience a change in his own body temperature unless that exposure is continued for a considerable period of time. An individual also can eat large amounts of one substance or another without greatly altering the composition of his or her own blood. This power to maintain a constant internal environment is known as *homeostasis* (from the Greek meaning "to keep a similar position"). The three-phased G.A.S. enables the body to maintain this constant internal environment in the face of various stressors.

Most of us have had the experience of lying in the hot summer sun in order to get a suntan. Although our reason for tanning is a cosmetic one, nature has something else in mind. Tanning is an example of adaptation designed to protect our tissues from the stress of ultraviolet light. The adaptive process therefore is essentially defensive in nature. And the degree to which the adaptation is stimulated is directly proportional to the intensity of the stressor. Have you ever attempted to get a tan in the middle of winter? You can lie in the sun for hours on end with little or no response. That's because the sun is not overhead during the winter and hence its rays are not very intense. What a difference when we're exposed to the hot midsummer sun—the body's response is immediate and dramatic! Initially there is a reddening and inflammation of the skin (the alarm stage of Selye's G.A.S). During this alarm stage the body gains time for the development and mobilization of specific adaptive phenomena. In this case the body marshals its store of melanin, or skin pigment, to be in readiness for further exposure to the sun's intense ultraviolet rays.

If exposure is repeated, adaptation moves into the stage of resistance. It's during this stage that overcompensation in the form of a tan takes place. But the energy involved in the adaptive process ("adaptation energy," as Selye refers to it) is limited, and if we prolong exposure to the intense sun we will swiftly enter the third stage of the G.A.S., exhaustion.

In the stage of exhaustion, the body's local reserves of adaptation energy are used up and the deep reserves of adaptation energy cannot be made available readily enough. Instead of overcompensating with a tan, we decompensate and lose tissue as blisters develop, then burns, and if exposure is continued long enough, death can occur.

So up to a certain point, exposure to the sun will result in overcompensation in the form of a tan. If exposure exceeds that duration, the body loses its ability to overcompensate and will decompensate instead. To stimulate the adaptive process, therefore, the stress to which we are exposed must be intense, but our exposure to such stress also must be brief and infrequent so that we don't deplete the reserves of adaptation energy that allow for overcompensation. You will note the implication of the principles of intensity, duration, and frequency with regard to the stress and the principles of identity and specificity with regard to the body's reaction to it.

"Weight training is a form of stress that we can control simply by varying the intensity, duration, and frequency of workouts."—Mike Mentzer

A PRACTICAL APPLICATION

Earlier I mentioned that while a state of stress can be induced by any number of stressors, making the cause nonspecific, the form it takes is always specific—and that form is the G.A.S.

Physical exercise is obviously a stressor. It's my belief that we can apply Selye's concept of the G.A.S. to our understanding of bodybuilding science and thereby make our bodybuilding training much more productive. The following is my plan for fashioning a training program around Selye's three stages of adaptation to stress:

The Alarm Stage

Just as exposure to the sun initially causes redness and inflammation, our first exposure to weight training (whether it's at the start of training or after a layoff) results in muscle soreness and general irritability. This alarm reaction is observed clinically and objectively as (in Selye's words) a "bodily expression of a generalized call to arms of the defensive forces in the organism," and it's unavoidable. While some soreness should be expected at first, such soreness does not have to be crippling. In *The Stress of Life* Selye says: "The alarm-response of the body is directly proportionate to the intensity of the aggression."

Extreme muscular soreness can be prevented by following a break-in period of training that is carefully designed to impose low-level stress in preparation for the more intense activity to come.

Beginners must be especially cautious. They should follow the suggested break-in routine listed below. Selye points out that during the acute phase of the alarm reaction, general resistance to the particular stressor actually falls below normal. That's because the body has not yet had sufficient time to mobilize its defensive forces against further assaults from the stressor.

During the alarm reaction the body's reduced general resistance is marked by a concentration of the blood and even a reduction in body weight. Curiously enough, this reduction of general resistance is similar to what happens to the body during the stage of exhaustion.

For beginners, an improper break-in routine could result in severe soreness and a loss of functional capacity (strength) and body weight. This could destroy motivation to continue. Even an experienced person, firm in the resolve to continue training, should go easy when resuming training after a layoff.

During the break-in period, which should last at least a week (depending on the individual's existing condition and innate adaptability), the beginner should perform the following routine every day for five consecutive days (please see Chapters 13 and 14 for explanations of how to perform these exercises):

1. Squats—1 set, 10 repetitions
2. Barbell rows—1 set, 10 repetitions
3. Bench press—1 set, 10 repetitions
4. Press behind neck—1 set, 10 repetitions
5. Deadlifts—1 set, 10 repetitions
6. Standing barbell curls—1 set, 10 repetitions
7. Standing calf raises—1 set, 10 repetitions
8. Sit-ups—1 set, 10 repetitions

These exercises should be performed with a weight that's light enough so you can complete 10 repetitions without extreme effort. Going to the point of exhaustion would increase the stress to a high level, making the symptoms of the alarm stage more severe. The idea here, Selye says, is merely to "mobilize the body's defensive forces" for further assaults and move the body into the stage of resistance. Inducing debilitating soreness is not necessary. While some soreness is unavoidable as part of the alarm reaction, it can be held in check if the exercises are not carried to the point of exhaustion.

If soreness persists after five days on this program, rest during the weekend and train again on Monday, Wednesday, and Friday. This time, however, perform two sets of each exercise. The first set should be performed just like the sets during the first week (same weight, reps, intensity, etc.). On the second set, increase the weight by 10 percent and try to perform 10 reps. Even with the greater weight, you should still be able to perform 10 reps, but, of course, a slightly greater effort will be required. This greater effort raises the stress level and thereby induces further adaptation. As Selye points out: "No living organism can be maintained continuously in a state of alarm."

If the stressor is not so intense that "continuous exposure to it is not compatible with life," the alarm reaction is followed by a second stage adaptation—the stage of resistance.

Again, the length of time a person needs to spend breaking in is contingent upon his existing physical condition and innate adaptability. If it takes only one week of such break-in training before you are ready to move on to more intense programs, fine. If, however, two weeks of such moderate break-in training still leaves you sore, stay with that moderate program for as long as necessary. Individuals who adapt this slowly are probably in very poor physical condition to start with and should have a thorough physical examination before starting a training program of any sort.

The Stage of Resistance

Please keep in mind that while a state of stress can be induced by any number of agents, the form it takes is always specific. This is true for every human being. I reiterate this because bodybuilders have been mistakenly led to believe that our response to exercise is totally individual. Lifting weights is a stress that's comparable to any other stress—the sun's rays, for example. Although it's true that some people respond more readily and to a greater extent to exercise (just as some acquire tans more rapidly and more deeply than do others) because of variation in innate adaptability, the factors underlying the process and mechanism of adaptive response are *exactly* the same in all human beings (the principle of identity again). So while it may be true that some may derive greater benefits from a given weight-training program than others, every person adapts and resists (by growing larger and stronger muscles) in proportion to the intensity of the stressor. Moreover, every human being who has ever lived possesses only limited reserves of local adaptation energy, which can slowly be restored from deeper stores during rest.

It is very difficult for us to control the intensity of the sun since that intensity is dependent on the seasons. But weight training is a form of stress that we can control simply by varying the intensity, duration, and frequency of workouts. When you go out into the hot July sun for the purpose of getting a suntan, you don't have to wait days, weeks, or months to see results. Response is immediate and dramatic. The same is true—or should be true—with weight training performed for the purpose of developing large, powerful muscles. Yet, amazingly, some misguided people have the mistaken notion that it takes years to develop even moderately.

To induce rapid and large-scale increases in muscular mass and strength, weight train-

Mike Mentzer was the first bodybuilder to understand and apply the General Adaptation Syndrome to bodybuilding.

ing must be intense. If it isn't, results will be slow—if there are any results at all. While some will gain more dramatically than others, even on a lower-intensity program, all individuals will respond more rapidly when the intensity of their training is as high as possible. Likewise, if an individual has had a fair measure of success on a program of moderate intensity, it means that he would have experienced far greater progress on a higher-intensity program. This is true for anyone.

While we adapt and respond to stress in proportion to its intensity, we also use up proportionate reserves of adaptation energy. In other words the greater the intensity, the more adaptation energy we use up. Selye never proved it clinically, but he believed that we possess local reserves of adaptation energy that are used up initially as we adapt to stress. This draining of the local reserves is what leads us to stop a bodybuilding workout at a certain point. These local stores can be replenished from deeper reserves elsewhere in the body when you rest between workouts.

Selye pointed out that such restoration of local reserves is slow. How slow? Well, you can tell by how well you're adapting to your workouts: are you getting bigger and stronger? You will recall that the first thing your body must do following a workout is restore its local reserves of adaptation energy. This will take place only if the workout was not so long that you used up too much of the reserve and if sufficient rest is allowed before the next workout. If your workouts are intense enough to stimulate a strong adaptive response, and the workouts are neither too long nor too close together, your body will overcompensate and grow larger and stronger.

If you have not experienced progress lately, there are three probable reasons:

1. The intensity was not high enough to stimulate a strong adaptive response.
2. The workouts were too long and the rest between them was too short to allow for overcompensation.
3. Your workouts were too low in intensity, too long, and too close together.

My advice to those who have experienced an impasse in their training progress is to first take a layoff of at least one full week. This should allow your body enough time to fully restore its reserves of adaptation energy. You'll need these reserves when you resume training on a higher-intensity program.

Your new program should consist of no more than two workouts a week, and you should do no more than two sets per bodypart. The low number of sets will enable you to generate maximum intensity of effort by going to complete failure on each and every set. If you do more sets than that, you will have to hold back somewhat on each set (i.e., pace your effort) so that you'll have enough energy and drive to complete the total number. While it may actually require something less than 100 percent effort to induce growth stimulation, how would you know what that level might be?

Continuing to exercise before the local reserves of adaptation energy have been replenished will result in your reaching a stage of exhaustion.

You couldn't, so be sure to pass the stimulation threshold point by going to 100 percent effort on each set.

If such a program of high-intensity training conducted two days a week does not produce immediate results, cut your workouts back to one workout every five to seven days instead. If the intensity is high and you're still not seeing progress, you are not allowing enough time between workouts. If you're not making progress and are not regressing either, then you are at least compensating for the stress of the workout, but obviously you're not overcompensating. (A complete high-intensity routine can be found in Chapter 13.)

The Stage of Exhaustion

As a high-intensity workout proceeds, we experience a reduction in drive. If we continue long enough, this reduction will become acute and exhaustion sets in so that we are forced to stop. When local reserves of adaptation energy are exhausted during exertion, they can be restored from a deeper source only by resting. Enough time must be allowed between workouts for full restoration of the local reserves. If not enough rest is taken and we continue our workouts by drawing from the deep reserves, the initial result will be a loss of muscle size and strength. Continuing further will produce a burned out feeling, accompanied by a strong disinclination to continue any type of physical activity. Selye contended that local or superficial adaptation energy is immediately available upon demand. Deep adaptation energy, however, is stored away safely as a reserve. The stage of exhaustion, after a temporary demand like a workout is reversible, but the exhaustion of our reserves of deep adaptation energy is not reversible. As these deep reserves are depleted in normal life, the result is senility and finally, death. While it's not very likely that anyone would carry overtraining to the point of death, we should at least know enough about the nature of adaptation by now to realize that our ability to successfully cope with the exhaustive effects of a workout are limited. If we are to make optimal progress, our workouts must be brief, intense, and properly spaced.

I hope that this explanation of the stress concept has made it clear that stress can be made to work for us. Stress can be good or bad, depending on how well we understand the relationship of intensity and duration. The chart below will clarify this idea:

This chart shows that up to a certain point, exposure to an intense stressor can result in the positive effect of overcompensation. Once exposure proceeds beyond that point, however, we are no longer able to successfully cope with the stress and we head in the exact opposite direction, decompensation. The above holds true for any form of stress. I simply chose the effects of the sun on our skin, friction on our palms, and exercise on our muscles because bodybuilders can easily identify with these.

As our training progresses over the years, we seem to invariably hit plateaus in our progress. Theoretically, sticking points should not occur if we apply our understanding of the principle of adaptation (G.A.S.) to our training; we should continue progressing until we reach the absolute limits of our potential. But most of us probably would not progress continuously even if we did apply such knowledge, because we're all subject to ups and downs in motivation—not to mention those inevitable pitfalls along life's way that occasionally force us to break training. As of yet no one has reached the outer limits of his or her potential.

However, if we can fully grasp the fact that training intensity must progress as we grow larger and stronger, we will continue adapting by growing still larger and stronger. As we fully adapt to a certain level of training intensity, we must increase the training intensity again if we wish to continue improving. Reaching the limits of our muscular potential, therefore, requires that we increase the intensity of our training notch by notch until we reach our limits of adaptation.

Stressor	Good Effect (Overcompensation)	Bad Effect (Decompensation)
Sun	Tan	Depletion, blisters, burns
Friction	Callus	Blisters, loss of tissue
Exercise	Gains in mass and strength	Loss of mass and strength

No bodybuilder has yet hit the upper reaches of his or her genetic potential—however, a more thorough understanding of the General Adaptation Syndrome will help to stave off plateaus and prevent overtraining.

A training journal is your only objective means to determine whether or not you are making progress in your workouts. Here Mike Mentzer (left) reviews the data in Aaron Baker's training journal to help him prepare for his next workout.

Chapter 10

THE SEVENTH PRINCIPLE
PROGRESSION

We now come to the final fundamental principle in the theory of high-intensity training—progression. The sixth principle revealed that one must be specific in one's training; that a certain type of training effort will yield a certain or specific type of training effect. We've learned from all of the preceding training principles that training must be of a high-intensity nature to stimulate a muscular increase, and that such training must be carried on neither too long nor conducted too frequently so as to prevent that increase. When the preceding six principles are understood, integrated, and applied properly, the seventh principle will look after itself.

Nevertheless, it helps to keep your eye on the one readily discernable index of whether your training efforts along with the duration and frequency of your workouts are having the desired effect. If not, then you must revisit these principles and honestly assess whether or not you are effectively employing them to the best of your ability. If you are, then you should witness progress in the form of an increase in strength; that is, an increase in reps, weight, or both from workout to workout.

Progress should not be an irregular, unpredictable phenomenon because there is no mystery to any of this. As we learned in Chapter 5 (The Second Principle: Intensity), the cause-and-effect relationship between exercise and the development of muscular mass beyond normal levels was established long ago with the research of physiologists such as Roux, Lange, Petow, Siebert, and Steinhaus. And because intensity of effort is the key and you want to keep your muscles growing, you will have to look for ways of increasing the intensity of your workouts on a progressive basis (a complete presentation of the various training principles I recommend to progressively increase the intensity of your workouts can be found in the next chapter).

Look at the principle of progression this way: if you want your muscles to grow progressively larger and stronger, then something about your workouts must progressively increase. This is where the great majority of

For your workouts to be progressive, your weights or repetitions—or both—must increase each and every workout.

"When we lift a barbell, we aren't just lifting a certain amount of weight; we are lifting that weight over a certain distance in a certain amount of time."—Mike Mentzer

bodybuilders become confused, even top bodybuilders. The common though mistaken notion is that progress is contingent upon duration. That is, as you grow and get stronger you will need to increase the amount of training. The obvious fallacy here is that as one progressed towards the upper limits of her size/strength potential, she might be training 10, 12, 20 hours a day. This would be impossible because, again, the body only has a limited ability to compensate for the effects of training stress.

In order to make your body grow progressively bigger and stronger, you must increase the intensity of your training. If you are not progressing, it is because you have adapted to a particular level of training intensity and further progress will not come until you up the intensity level. This is the nature of the body's

adaptive ability. You must impose an extraordinary demand upon the muscles to stimulate the adaptive response.

Size and strength increases signal that the intensity of your training efforts was sufficient to tax your physical reserves. Because the body's reserves are limited, the body will enlarge upon its normal abilities so that future assaults of high-intensity training won't use them all up. As you grow stronger, the same amount of intensity will use up less of your reserves and stave off the possibility of eventual death. In time progress will halt altogether as you adapt to a particular intensity level— which must be the case. For many, the dilemma of inducing more progress is not knowing or understanding the nature of adaptation. For the beginner who has never trained, any type of training represents a big step up the ladder of intensity. Even mild calisthenics would prove sufficiently intense to stimulate an adaptation towards bigger and stronger muscles. Not for long, however. Soon more intensity would be required for more progress. This can easily be supplied with the added resistance provided by barbells and a basic routine. This step up the ladder of intensity will again stimulate more size and strength increases until full adaptation occurs. And so one must climb progressively up the ladder of intensity to the dizzying and frightening heights of one's ultimate size and strength potential.

WEIGHT, DISTANCE, AND TIME

When we lift a barbell, we aren't just lifting a certain amount of weight; we are lifting that weight over a certain distance in a certain amount of time. The three factors (or essential components) are weight, distance, and time. If we wish to increase our individual training intensity, then we must cause our muscles to generate more horsepower. This is accomplished by lifting heavier weights over greater distances in shorter periods of time. Adjusting the amount of weight we lift in any particular exercise is the easiest factor to understand and apply to our workouts. Whenever there is an increase in strength, the amount of weight used in that exercise should be increased. If you can currently bench press 250 pounds for six maximum repetitions and two weeks from now you can bench press the same weight for 10 maximum reps, the weight should be increased by approximately 5 to 10 percent, or whatever amount is required to lower your maximum rep performance to six once again. Still later, when you can do 10 reps with the heavier weight, increase the poundage another 5 to 10 percent. Keep increasing the weight as you increase your strength. Such is the nature of the principle of progression (i.e., progressive weight-resistance exercise).

Since the lengths of our bones are fixed, there isn't much we can do to increase the distance over which we move the weights in most of our exercises. The distance you move a weight in the barbell curl, for instance, is directly related to the length of your forearms. And unless you are young and still growing, that distance, for all intents and purposes, will remain fixed and unalterable.

Lifting weights in shorter periods of time is a relatively simple matter but subject to some misunderstanding. In speaking of the speed on an isolated repetition, the weight should be moved from a position of full extension to one of full contraction in the shortest possible time, utilizing only the force of muscular contraction. In reality, this turns out to be a relatively slow movement, especially if the weight is heavy. When the speed exceeds a certain

The distance you move a weight in the barbell curl is directly related to the length of your forearms.

Rest only long enough in between sets to catch your breath, so that each set is taken to a point of muscular failure—rather than cardiovascular failure.

rate, momentum takes over and is responsible for completing the movement. And remember that intensity refers to muscular contraction. Momentum is an outside force that will diminish intensity if you're not careful. All your exercises therefore should be initiated deliberately, with no sudden thrusts or jerks, and carried to completion relatively slowly, with the weight always under control.

When referring to the amount of time between sets, only rest long enough so you can resume with enough efficiency to carry the next set to muscular failure. If rest time is too brief, your next set will terminate at a point of cardiovascular failure instead of muscular failure. And if the rest is too long, the muscle will cool off, preventing maximum effort.

EXERCISING YOUR WILL

Simply manipulating the variables cited above isn't the whole picture as far as increasing intensity goes; there also exists a very strong mental barrier to inducing greater and greater muscular contractions—and with good reason: A very large and strong muscle contracting with maximum intensity places much greater demands on the body's recuperative subsystems than does a smaller, weaker one. Because these demands upon the body's resources are potentially life threatening, your mind as well as your body will do everything possible to prevent such taxing high-intensity exertion.

Lassitude, anxiety, and even a preference for low-intensity workouts are manifestations of the mind's disinclination to engage the body in such maximal efforts. Therefore, as your muscles get stronger and stronger, you must exercise your will to get stronger apace. Having been successful in my efforts to become both muscularly massive and very strong, I can assure you that the principle of intensity refers almost exclusively to the human will and the ability to command your muscles to contract against the only real resistance—your own mind.

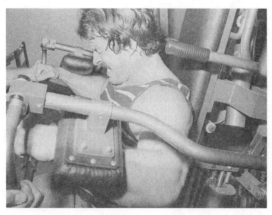

"The principle of intensity refers almost exclusively to the human will and the ability to command your muscles to contract against the only real resistance—your own mind."—Mike Mentzer

High-intensity training is hard training, and as such it has a definite effect on our physiologic systems. This effect can be measured in the lab and felt subjectively by the individual doing the training. The effect is dramatic and can be very uncomfortable. Whereas rest and total inactivity are experienced as comfortable, training at maximum intensity is brutal and uncomfortable. If you are able to talk between sets and feel the desire to add more sets to your workouts, then you're not training with maximum intensity. If you are training with maximum effort, you won't be able to talk between sets because you'll be breathing too hard. And instead of thinking about doing more sets, you'll begin looking for excuses to *shorten* your workouts.

INTENSITY IS RELATIVE

While a high intensity of effort is necessary for anyone wishing to build muscle, and its effects are similar on everyone, intensity remains a relative measure, contingent upon an individual's existing level of strength and development. Let's face it, a 12-inch arm contracting maximally will not require the same amount of fuel or produce the same quantities of by-products and wastes as a 20-inch arm contracting maximally. Since we require increasingly greater contractions if we hope to continually progress, we must search for increasingly more intense methods to provide such contractions as we get stronger.

For the beginner, just about any form of resistance exercise will represent an increase in intensity to his overall system. As he progresses to the intermediate and advanced stage, however, he will require increasingly more intense training methods. If you are presently experiencing little or no progress with your current training routine, stop it immediately, as it is probably not intense enough to stimulate muscle growth. Employ the above points with respect to increasing the intensity of your workouts and you will soon be growing again.

And while you should expect strength increases regularly if you train properly, not everyone achieves a regular or attendant

Mentzer was the type of individual who gained muscle mass cyclically; first he would gain strength, and then he would gain the mass.

"Progress should be immediate and significant from the time you start using a routine, and it should be continuous from that point on."—Mike Mentzer

increase in muscular mass or bodyweight. For the majority, strength increases precede size increases. So you will gain in strength for a time without seeing much in the way of a meaningful size increase. I don't want to mislead anyone on this crucial point, which is important to understand from a motivational standpoint. As you continue to gain in strength, your strength increases will eventually yield an increase in muscular mass. Just how much muscle you gain and how long it takes is, as we learned in Chapter 2, dictated by genetics.

I was the type of individual who gained muscle mass cyclically. I remember numerous stretches during which my strength increased regularly for up to several months without an accompanying mass increase. Not realizing then that strength increases often precede size increases, I would often become frustrated. I was tempted to give up training entirely more than once, but I persisted and in time my per-

sistence would always be rewarded as my burgeoning strength always yielded an appreciable mass increase. I've observed this same pattern of response in many of my personal training clients. They will gain regularly in strength for months with little or no increase in size, and then within a short period of time they'll find themselves several pounds heavier.

People often ask me if they will see results in six months using my high-intensity training system. I tell them they won't have to wait six months: They will see results immediately from the first workout. Progress should be immediate and significant from the time you start using a routine, and it should be continuous from that point on. It is my experience in training thousands of bodybuilders that one should be able to reach the limits of one's genetic potential within one year of proper training—if the seven principles of high-intensity training are followed faithfully.

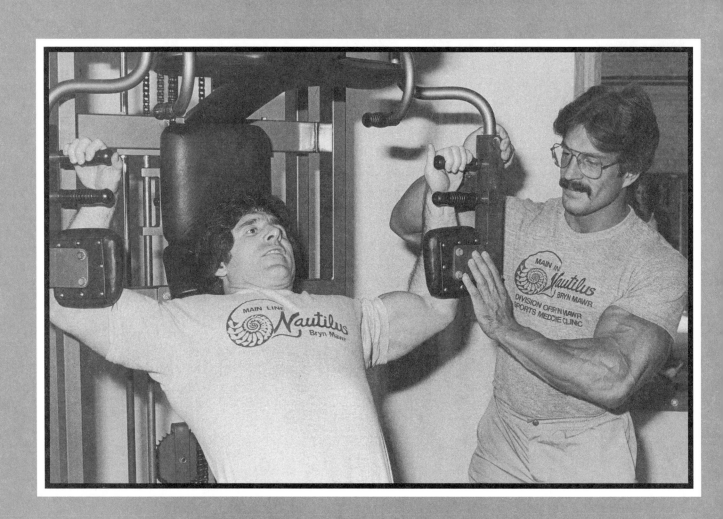

Part III

DERIVATIVES

Mentzer applied all of the high-intensity training principles in this chapter at one time or another over the course of his bodybuilding career.

Chapter 11

A COMPENDIUM OF HIGH-INTENSITY TRAINING PRINCIPLES

It's fairly obvious that to build big muscles and increase your strength, you must lift weights. But the number of letters I get from bodybuilders asking me how they can build bigger arms, rounder pecs, thicker delts, and so forth, shows that what isn't so obvious is *how* to lift those weights and *what kinds* of workouts one should do in order to build big muscles.

Those who read Chapters 4–10 of this book have hopefully come away from them with the firm understanding that only by generating progressively stronger muscular contractions do we build muscle tissue. What remains obscure to so many bodybuilders, as evidenced by the many questions I receive, is how to progressively increase the intensity of their muscular contractions. This obscurity arises in part from the fact that many still do not fully understand the concept of intensity.

Intensity is a term that has been bandied about a lot lately in all the bodybuilding periodicals. Very rarely, however, is intensity described accurately. It's obvious when reading the various articles that the authors—including certain top bodybuilders—still confuse intensity with duration. Apparently the authors in these cases have not grasped the fundamental relationship that exists between the two. As hopefully we have learned by now, intensity and duration are, for one thing, mutually exclusive. Only when a muscle is contracting with the greatest possible force at any given moment is there maximum intensity. When you're training in such a way that every rep of every set of every exercise requires an absolute maximum effort, the duration of that workout must be and will be brief. High-intensity muscular contraction, in other words, prevents a large number of such contractions.

So maximum training intensity limits the duration of your training. What's even more significant is that anything less than maximum intensity will result in less than optimal results. Arthur Jones once told me that he likened exercise and muscle growth to a stick of dynamite and a hammer. Hitting a stick of dynamite lightly with a hammer will not produce an explosion no matter how many times you hit it.

Going from low- to high-intensity activity—whether in weight training or sprinting—represents a huge change in the metabolism and energy systems of the body.

If, however, you hit it very hard, only one blow is required to stimulate or produce an explosion.

Much the same situation exists in stimulating growth with weight training. No amount of light or low-intensity training will produce an increase. High-intensity training is a basic requirement in producing the desired physical change. Large quantities of such stimulation are not necessary, nor are they desired. In other words, it takes only one hard blow from the hammer to set off the explosion of the dynamite.

Personal experience has taught most of us that high-intensity training produces an effect on our bodies that we never get from low-intensity work. The effect that training of different intensity levels has upon our systems can be better understood if we look at an intensity continuum (see page 87) in which complete inactivity and rest constitute one extreme and

absolute, all-out effort constitutes the other. The effect each extreme has on our system is obviously very different.

These are just four indices registering the change in our systems when we go from a state of rest to one of all-out effort. Of course, there are many more indices, such as pH and lactic acid levels, but you get the idea.

In Chapter 10 I touched on some of the factors that must be factored into any training technique or principle if it is to result in an increase in the intensity of any given exercise: that the amount of weight lifted, the amount of time it takes to lift the weight, and the rest time between sets determines intensity. Distance will be a fixed value, not subject to adjustment (at least on conventional equipment). The following training principles are based on these simple features and if applied correctly, they will definitely enhance your progress.

Continuum of Intensity	
Rest/Total Inactivity	Maximum Effort
(lowest possible intensity)	(highest possible intensity)
Pulse rate: slow, 60–75 beats per minute	Pulse rate: fast, 150–220 beats per minute
Breathing: shallow and slow	Breathing: very rapid
(12–14 breaths per minute)	(50–100 breaths per minute)
O₂ uptake (ventilation-oxygen uptake ratio): 20–25	O₂ uptake: 30
Respiratory Exchange Index (Energy exchange within body; a partial measure of body metabolism): 0.825	Respiratory Exchange Index: 1.20

TRAINING TO FAILURE

Putting aside all academic and theoretical considerations for a moment, what we are talking about here, quite simply, is hard work—gutbusting, all-out effort! Any degree of effort below maximum may yield the bodybuilder some results but never on the same order as all-out effort. And, again, when I say "all-out effort," I'm not referring to the performance of marathon workouts involving set after set after set until you fall over from fatigue.

Training to a point of momentary muscular failure, at which the completion of another full rep is impossible despite your greatest effort, is the only way to force the body to resort to its reserves sufficiently to stimulate

"What we are talking about here, quite simply, is hard work." Mentzer gives his all to a set of Nautilus shoulder presses.

real growth. None of us needs to be reminded that growth never comes easy; it must literally be *forced*. Ending a set just because an arbitrary number of reps has been completed will do little or nothing to stimulate growth. If you can curl 100 pounds for 10 reps and you never try to do that eleventh rep, your body has no reason to alter itself, to grow. The body will always attempt to maintain the existing situation. Only when you impose some extraordinary demand upon it will it change. You needn't be a physiologist to understand that.

Carrying a set to a point of momentary muscular failure ensures that you pass through the *break-over point*—the level of effort in the set at which growth stimulation commences. Where is that point? Is it at 85 percent of maximum effort? Is it at 90 percent? No one knows for sure, but you can be certain that if you train at 100 percent effort, you will have reached the break-over point.

For those who are just taking up weight training, I suggest you proceed with caution at first. If you have been sedentary most of your life, weight training will represent a radical departure for you. Training to absolute failure may not only be unnecessary but dangerous. The first several months should be spent learning proper exercise form and developing a sense of your capacities.

As you develop confidence in handling weights and you gain added muscle and strength, start carrying each and every set (not including warm-up sets) to a point of momen-

Carrying a set to the point of muscular failure—when another rep is impossible despite your greatest effort—is what ensures growth stimulation.

tary muscular failure. Select a weight in each exercise that will allow approximately six reps in strict form. Maximum reps in strict form means going to a point where you can no longer raise the weight in perfectly strict fashion from a point of complete extension to one of full contraction. Everyone wishing to induce maximum muscle growth should follow this method of training to failure.

PRE-EXHAUSTION

As mentioned above, it's imperative that we pass through the break-over point in intensity by carrying each set to a point of momentary failure. This is impossible, however, on exercises involving two or more muscles when one of these is a so-called weak link.

Most conventional weight exercises for the chest, for example, involve the triceps. The

triceps, being a smaller and, therefore, weaker muscle, will prevent you from working the pectorals to a point of failure. If you can incline 200 pounds for six reps, it's not the pectorals that are preventing you from lifting more weight or doing more reps; it's the weaker triceps giving out first.

A similar situation exists when we work the latissimus dorsi (lat) muscles of the upper back with conventional rowing, chinning, or pulldown movements. The biceps are unavoidably involved in these exercises because the upper arms must bend. Since the biceps are smaller and weaker than the much larger latissimus muscles, they will give out first, preventing the lat muscles from being worked to the maximum and receiving full growth stimulation.

This situation can be remedied by first performing an exercise that isolates and tires the primary muscle group. For example, cable

Machines such as the Nautilus behind neck machine provide resistance directly to the lat muscles, bypassing the smaller and weaker biceps muscles that typically give out in compound exercises for the lats such as barbell rows, chin-ups, and pulldowns.

crossovers, dumbbell flyes, and Nautilus flyes serve to isolate the pecs. By carrying one of these exercises to a point of failure and then proceeding immediately to an exercise that involves the pecs along with a secondary muscle—say, the triceps, in the case of the chest—the triceps will have a temporary strength advantage over the pre-exhausted pectoral muscles. This will serve to enhance your chest work rather than hinder it.

This will only be the case, however, as long as there is zero rest between the first isolation exercise and the second compound exercise (a compound exercise is one in which more than one muscle group is used to move the resistance). Taking any more rest than the time it takes to move from one piece of equipment to the other will seriously compromise the effectiveness of this method as the pre-exhausted muscle will regain up to 50 percent of its strength within three to five seconds of completion of the set!

Examples of pre-exhaust exercise sequences follow:

Pecs

Flyes and bench presses
Cable crossovers and dips
Pec decks and incline presses

Lats

Dumbbell pullovers and barbell rows
Nautilus pullovers and chins (palms up)
Straight-arm pulldowns and regular pulldowns (palms up)

Delts

Dumbbell laterals and presses behind neck
Nautilus laterals and nautilus presses

Traps

> Shrugs (barbell, dumbbell, Nautilus) and upright rows

Thighs

> Leg extensions and leg presses or squats

Triceps

> Pressdowns and dips
> French presses and close-grip bench presses

Biceps

> Barbell curls and close-grip, palms-up pulldowns
> Nautilus curls and palms-up chins

Note: In training the triceps and biceps, the pecs and lats aren't weak links. But compound exercises involving the latter two muscles can help the triceps and biceps continue working after being fatigued by an isolation exercise.

Tips on Using Pre-Exhaust

1. Keep the reps fairly low in a pre-exhaust superset since you are doing two consecutive sets. Too many reps—more than 10—can lead to labored breathing and could prevent you from continuing the exercise until muscular failure is reached. Six strict reps is best.
2. Never perform more than two pre-exhaust cycles or supersets.
3. Beginners don't necessarily require pre-exhaust. Intermediates and advanced bodybuilders can add forced reps and negatives to either one or both of the exercises in the pre-exhaust cycle.
4. Don't get stuck on using pre-exhaust or any other method exclusively. Using pre-exhaust once a week for each bodypart is sufficient.

PEAK CONTRACTION TRAINING

As we must generate progressively stronger muscular contractions to stimulate maximum increases in size and strength, two conditions must be met: (1) since muscle fibers contract by reducing their length, a muscle would have to be in the fully contracted, or peak, position if all the fibers were to be contracted simultaneously; (2) to get all the fibers contracted at the same time, one would have to impose a load that was intense enough to activate all of the muscle's fibers.

When a muscle moves against a heavy resistance through a full range of motion (from a position of full extension to one of complete contraction), more and more fibers come into play until peak contraction is reached. At peak contraction no further movement is possible and the maximum number of fibers have been activated. The peak contraction principle comes into play in those exercises that provide resistance in the peak contraction position, the most important point in the range of motion of any exercise.

In choosing the best exercises for peak contraction, select those that make you struggle to hold the weight at the top. The regular barbell curl is a poor exercise (unless it's angled) because once you pass mid-range, the effective resistance falls off dramatically. Exercises such as leg extensions, tricep pressdowns, chins, and various Nautilus movements provide resistance in the contracted position, allowing for a higher intensity of contraction when sufficient weight is handled. When formulating a routine, select at least one exercise for each bodypart that involves this important principle.

FORCED REPETITIONS

Anything you do to make your training harder—not longer, but more brutal moment to moment—will raise the intensity and the effectiveness of your workouts. After you've reached a point of failure where another strict rep is impossible despite the greatest effort, you can increase the intensity still more by having your training partner assist you in the completion of two or three forced reps. In most cases, it's best to keep the same weight on the bar and have your partner assist you just enough so that

The Nautilus rear delt machine provides resistance through a full range of motion, most importantly in the position of peak contraction, in which the elbows are drawn back as far as they will go.

you can barely complete the rep with all-out, gut-busting effort.

Many people write me asking if reducing the weight and completing several more reps is just as good. The answer is no. If you reduce the weight too much, the next rep will not require maximum, all-out effort, so the intensity actually will fall below the level of the last strict rep you completed on your own. Keeping the weight the same and getting just enough assistance from a partner who is in tune with you assures an increase in intensity.

Forced reps aren't necessary for beginners for reasons already discussed. Intermediates might add forced reps to one of the exercises in the pre-exhaust sequence, either the isolation exercise or the compound movement. Advanced bodybuilders probably would do well to try forced reps on both the isolation and compound exercises of that sequence. I wouldn't recommend doing forced reps every workout necessarily, especially for intermedi-

ates. Intermediates should take each bodypart to positive failure in one workout, to positive failure with forced reps the next workout, and to negative failure in the third workout.

The advanced bodybuilder who requires higher intensity and is more in tune with his physical needs should play it by ear. An advanced person may want to depart from the suggested rep protocol of six strict positive reps followed by forced reps. Since his larger and stronger muscles place much greater demands on his cardio-respiratory and other physical systems during very heavy contraction, he may want to use weights that only allow a maximum of four strict positive reps. It's a matter of using one's judgment.

NEGATIVE REPETITIONS

You may recall that our skeletal muscles possess three types of strength:

Mike *(left)* and Ray Mentzer *(right)* provide some added assistance to a trainee struggling to complete his set of heavy machine incline presses. A little bit of upward pressure will allow the trainee to push the resistance through a sticking point in the range of motion, allowing him to force out several extra repetitions.

Mentzer pulls the triceps bar down to the fully contracted position, allowing Aaron Baker to concentrate on the negative portion of the triceps pushdown exercise.

1. Positive strength, or the ability to raise a weight.
2. Static, or holding, strength.
3. Negative strength, or our ability to lower a weight.

We are weakest in positive strength and strongest in negative strength. Obviously, we can't really say we've trained to failure until we've also exhausted our ability to lower the weight. Only by continuing to lower a weight after completing six positive reps and two forced reps—which will exhaust your positive and static strength levels—can you reach a point of true and absolute momentary muscular failure.

Having completed your six positives and two forced reps, have your partner, or partners, lift the weight to the top (or peak contracted position) so that you can lower it. You'll probably be surprised at your ability to continue

lowering a weight even after you've reached positive failure. The first few negatives will seem very easy and you'll be able to lower the weight slowly. The next couple of reps will become difficult, however. The downward movement will pick up speed, and you won't have as much control.

End the set when you can no longer control the descent of the weight, or stop a rep prior to that, as a heavy weight yanking a bodypart out of the contracted position can be dangerous. On certain exercises involving large and powerful muscles, like the thighs, be very careful. I would advise against doing squats in this manner for obvious safety reasons, and even thigh extensions can be dangerous.

You may find that the weight you used for six positive reps will be too light for continued negatives. If that's the case, your partner will have to apply manual resistance as you lower

At the end of a regular set of Nautilus lateral raises, a training partner helps Mentzer lift the movement arms of the machine into the fully contracted position in which Mentzer must then resist the downward pull of the weights all on his own.

the weight. Do not—I repeat, *do not*—attempt to halt the downward motion of the weight when you're doing negatives. The knees tend to be delicate. If you fight against a maximum negative resistance, you could cause severe injury to the knees.

Beginners don't require negatives as it is a high-intensity method reserved for ambitious intermediate and advanced bodybuilders. Negatives also can be done in a so-called pure style; i.e., they don't have to be preceded by positive and forced reps. Take a weight that's at least 40 percent heavier than you would normally use in positive fashion, have spotters raise it for you, and continue lowering the weight slowly until you're beginning to lose control. Make sure your spotters remain alert to what you're doing so they can grab the weight as soon as you signal for them to do so.

Entire workouts can be done in this fashion or combined with positive and forced reps as described earlier. Be innovative and improvise. The isolation portion of a pre-exhaust superset can be done positive/forced/ negative fashion and the compound exercise of the same superset in negative style only, for example.

There are limitless combinations and ways of employing all these methods so that no two workouts need be the same. I would advise against using negatives in every workout. Since the intensity is so high, it could lead to overtraining.

REST-PAUSE TRAINING

As we climb steadily up the ladder of intensity, the demand for more brutal workouts increases. The problem for the advanced bodybuilder is compounded by mitigating physiological changes that accompany high growth and strength increases. A large and strong muscle contracting intensely and consecutively creates a profound oxygen debt and waste product buildup. As a matter of fact, total oxygen uptake in a muscle working at maximum capacity may increase 30 times! Muscle contractions can, however, become so intense that blood flow—and hence oxygen delivery—is

Rest-pause requires you to perform one full repetition with a very heavy weight. Then, after a 10-second rest, the weight would be reduced to allow you to perform another all-out repetition. This type of training is as productive as it is intense.

decreased. In effect then, more time has to be allowed between contractions, or reps, for the vascular system to fill before the next contraction; thus, the principle of rest-pause training.

Further scientific evidence backing up the basis for rest-pause training can be found in the fine exercise physiology textbook by Edington and Edgerton entitled *The Biology of Physical Exercise.* As stated in the book: "Blood flow to working muscles does not increase at high work intensities when the duration of contractions is short enough, and the duration of relaxation is long enough."

The bodybuilder can overcome the diminished capacity for continued high-intensity contraction by resting up to 10 seconds between reps. This rest-pause will allow blood to bring fuel to the working muscle, as well as

rid the muscle of the metabolic by-products. My use of this method involved the selection of a weight that allowed for one maximum rep in a particular exercise. After performing that one rep, I'd put the weight down, rest for 10 seconds and then do another rep. Usually by the second or third rep, I'd have to reduce the weight by 10 percent or have my partner provide just enough assistance to allow another maximum effort.

I would do one set of four reps for each exercise. Never did I do more than three total sets per bodypart. I experimented at first by resting 15 seconds between reps. Other times I rested for seven seconds. Fifteen turned out to be too long and seven seconds too short. I also tried six reps per set, but I found it too taxing and it immediately led to overtraining. Doing four reps, with the 10-second rest-pause, I increased every single exercise at least 20 pounds per workout until I finally had improved 66 percent on each one. My size, of course, increased also.

Beginners and intermediates should save this training method for later in their bodybuilding careers when they need it. Advanced bodybuilders might want to experiment a bit with rest times and number of reps as I did. Keep in mind, however, that this is one of the most intense and brutal methods of training ever devised! Keep your sets low, and if progress is not immediately and dramatically forthcoming, you have exceeded your body's ability to cope with this intense form of stress—you're overtraining. You must realize that unlike the other methods of training where you perform one maximum effort per set, in rest-pause training every rep is maximum. While such effort is highly productive, it is also very, very taxing. Beware!

PARTIAL REPETITIONS

For upcoming bodybuilders whose continuation in the lifestyle relies heavily on consistent feedback that his or her efforts are returning increased size and strength, a routine revolving around heavy full and partial reps on basic exercises in the power rack is indicated.

Advanced bodybuilders, who have enough critical mass to consider entering competition, are not as obsessed with making quantum increases in overall muscular size. Their primary concern is to perfect their hard-earned muscular foundation by filling in the gaps and bringing weak parts up to parity with the whole. For these individuals use of partial-range exercise must be more specific. By the time a bodybuilder reaches the competitive level he or she is only too painfully aware of weak points. In a well-intended but misguided effort to correct the weak parts, most bodybuilders merely add exercises and sets to their existing regimes. Since most bodybuilders are already overtraining, such an increase in the

Heavy partial movements such as squats are best performed in a power rack or a Smith machine, of which the safety bars can be set to not only restrict your range of motion, but catch the weight if you descend too deep.

volume of training will necessitate a decrease in intensity, a further depletion of their recuperative reserves, less results, more frustration, and the increased likelihood of ceasing training altogether.

The proper approach, of course, to overcoming weak points is not an increase in the amount of work performed but an increase in the intensity of effort. Increased intensity must be attended by a decrease in the duration of the workout or the growth that was stimulated won't occur. I have found that an extremely effective method to quickly up one's intensity output is the principle of partial repetitions with a weight that is much heavier than what I

Mentzer was phenomenally strong in the partial squat movement, working up to well over 1,000 pounds. However, he would later advise that it was not necessary to employ that much weight and to use the technique only sparingly.

would typically utilize with a full-range movement in the same exercise. With this method the lifter performs partial reps only from the mid-range or halfway point in the exercise. In all of your exercises the amount of resistance you handle is limited by the weakest point in the range of motion. For example, the mid-range of a barbell curl is hardest. But because of leverage changes through the range of motion, the effective resistance of the weight on the bar being curled increases to its maximum at the midpoint, whereupon it immediately decreases. The midpoint of a curl is the weakest range, and the amount of weight used is limited by your midrange strength.

The limitations to how much resistance can be used in an exercise can be overcome by performing certain exercises that extend only to the midpoint. The poundage and the effective overload will rise dramatically. When training for the Mr. Universe contest with my brother Ray as my training partner, I started performing half-reps on the incline press with a relatively close grip to fill in a weak point I had in the upper pecs. While my usual full-range presses were performed with 315 to 365 pounds at the most, mid-range incline presses allowed me to handle 405 to 455 pounds. Such an overload caused my upper pecs to fill out quickly because of the increased intensity.

These mid-range reps were only an adjunct to my usual full-range performance on all exercises. The mid-range exercises were performed for two sets each for each bodypart. Don't make the mistake of not using full-range exercise; both are absolute requirements for complete development!

We also used mid-range exercises to develop our biceps and thighs. Once we finished our usual three maximum-intensity full-range sets for biceps, Ray and I would overload the bar for Scott (Preacher) curls from our usual 150 pounds for full-range reps to 220 pounds for mid-range reps. Using a Scott bench perpendicular to the ground so the resistance didn't fall off in the top of the movement, one of us would lower the 220-pound bar to the halfway position, where the other's hands would stop the bar and possibly even give a slight boost to get the mammoth weight started back upward. Once the weight began its ascent no assistance was given. About five reps performed in this all-out fashion were all we could take. After a set performed in said manner we'd immediately sit down to avoid falling down! When working our thighs we'd do our typical maximum pre-exhaustion cycle of leg extensions followed immediately by the leg press. Then after a few minutes rest and a gradual warm-up for the lower back with lighter squats, Ray and I would perform one or two sets of mid-range squats for up to 800 pounds in the power rack.

The principle of partial repetitions can be used on any bodypart that might be lagging. Ray and I used it for our pecs, thighs, and biceps as we thought those areas needed a little touch-up work at the time. I strongly advise once again that partials serve merely as an adjunct to your usual full-range work. Because of the added overload it imposes on the lagging muscle it can produce immediate results but only if not overdone. Restrict partial repetitions to those bodyparts that might be lagging and perform only one exercise for no more than one set per bodypart! Used properly, the principle of partial repetitions will prove a spark that rekindles your progress and enthusiasm. Give it your all and the rewards will be commensurate.

STATIC CONTRACTION

Technically a bodybuilder is a bodybuilder, not a weightlifter. As a bodybuilder, your primary goal is not to lift heavy weights per se, but to achieve high-intensity muscular contractions as a means of inducing optimal growth stimulation. While it is true that to grow larger muscles one must increase his strength, such is not a bodybuilder's main purpose. A bodybuilder lifts progressively heavier weights in order to progressively increase the stress (intensity) of his workouts—a prerequisite for growing progressively larger muscles. For the bodybuilder, in other words, lifting weights is the means, not the end.

The science of productive bodybuilding exercise starts with a study and understanding of the nature of full, or high-intensity, muscular contractions (the principle of identity). And when we study the nature of muscle tissue, we learn that muscles perform work by contracting (reducing their length), and that muscles contract in an all-or-nothing fashion, which means that only the number of muscle fibers required to move a resistance are recruited, and these contract with 100 percent of their contractile ability. It's not that all of the fibers of a given muscle contract a little bit. No, only that percentage of the muscle's total fibers that are required, and these contract with 100 percent of their momentary ability: all or none.

Since muscles perform work by contracting, the only position where a muscle could be fully contracted would be in the fully contracted position, but only if sufficient resistance is imposed in the fully contracted position. In order to achieve optimal growth stimulation, a muscle would have to undergo a maximum, high-intensity contraction. This could only be achieved as a result of providing a muscle with a resistance sufficient to cause a full contraction of the muscle in the fully contracted position, such as at the top of a curl, the straight-leg, lock-kneed position of a leg extension, the contracted positions of the pulldown or pec deck, etc. It is not cast in stone that a bodybuilder must limit himself merely to lifting weights. Remember, the skeletal muscles all have three levels of ability, the second level of which is the static, or holding of the weight at any point in the range of motion such as the top, fully contracted position; static strength is considerably greater than positive strength.

The degree of growth stimulation is related to the degree of inroad into functional ability. When a person trains to positive failure, it might be said he made only one-third of an inroad into functional ability; therefore, he stimulated one-third of possible growth. By holding a weight in the fully contracted position to static failure and then finishing with a single negative, the degree of inroad into functional ability would be greater with greater growth stimulation. However, the greater the degree of inroad into functional ability, the greater the inroad into recovery ability; there-

Static contractions require you to take the muscle into a fully contracted position and hold it there statically for as long as possible. Here Mentzer reveals the peak position for static contractions in the seated calf raise exercise—look at that calf!

Mentzer reveals the fully contracted position of the Preacher curl exercise. Once the resistance has been raised to this position, the trainee must hold it through the strength of muscular contraction alone.

fore, a decrease in the number of sets may be required to compensate for that greater inroad.

I have many of my in-the-gym clients shift the focus of their efforts from lifting the weights to failure to holding the weights to failure in the fully contracted position, then lowering under strict negative control. I reasoned: since the fully contracted position is the only position where a full contraction could be achieved, and the weight that one can handle there is limited by how much his weaker positive strength can get into that position, let's eliminate the lifting of the weight entirely. I'll help my client into the contracted position with a weight heavier than he would handle for positive reps, and he'll hold that weight until he reaches a point of failure, i.e., until his static strength is exhausted. Then, as he notes his

static strength is about to go, he starts a slow, controlled negative, the lowering of the weight.

One of my regular gym clients improved his ability on the leg extension such that in a very short period of time he went from 190 pounds for seven positive reps to 250 pounds (the entire weight stack) for 14 positive reps. He then remained stuck for three workouts at 250 pounds for 14 reps, whereupon I had him do three leg workouts in a row of only holding the weight stack of 250 pounds in the straight-leg, lock-knee position to failure and, then, lowering slowly. In the first of these static workouts he held the stack for about 15 seconds in the lock-knee position, the second workout for 22 seconds, and in the third workout he held for about 30 seconds. The next leg workout, I had him do conventional positive

The leg extension exercise is ideal for static contraction training.

reps to see if there was a carryover, and he performed 20 full-range positive reps! Quite an improvement indeed.

Now I have most of my clients perform fully contracted static holds to failure followed immediately by a negative on those exercises that permit it—and the results are stunning, to say the least. I ascribe my clients' greater progress recently, in part, to the holds making a greater inroad into existing strength than do positives. With conventional high-intensity training, where a set is carried to positive failure, the inroad made into existing ability is nominal compared to a set carried with a heavier weight to holding failure—including a negative. Why? Because, as stated earlier, the positive (or raising) strength is your weakest level. Training to positive failure leaves considerable static and negative strength intact.

As with the Peak Contraction Principle, the exercises where this technique may be employed most successfully are isolation exercises, those involving rotary movement around one joint axis, and that provide resistance in the fully contracted position. For example: the pec deck; machine lateral raises; the leg extension and leg curl; and the calf raise. The one compound exercise with which I've used static holds is the close-grip, palms-up pulldown. The best machines to use are Nautilus since they were designed to provide full-range variable resistance with close to perfect resistance in the fully contracted position. For most exercises for which I have my training clients do fully contracted holds, I select a weight that is sufficiently heavy so they can hold it in the fully contracted position for a maximum of approximately 8 to 12 seconds for upper body

The close-grip, palms-up pulldown is another great exercise on which to employ the static contraction principle.

exercises and 15 to 30 seconds on lower body exercises; then they have to lower it under strict control.

In the beginning I had my clients perform two holds with two negatives (lowerings), but now I have found they do better with one hold and negative, and at times, rather than have them perform the holds without the positives, I vary their workouts and have them perform a set to positive failure followed immediately by a hold to failure. And this has worked out very well.

The proper progressive application of these training principles to your high-intensity training program will allow you to grow stronger with every single workout, without any breach in such progress, until you have reached the upper limits of your genetic potential.

The Herculean physique of Mike Mentzer is positive proof of the efficacy of the principles of high-intensity training.

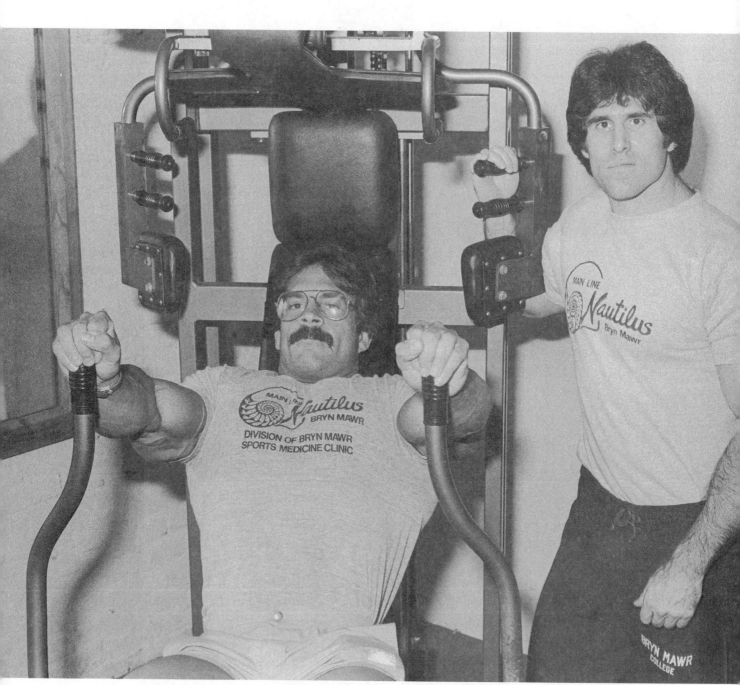

Mike Mentzer was a longtime advocate of both free weights and machines throughout his career. His favorite exercise machines were made by Nautilus.

Chapter 12

FREE WEIGHTS VS. MACHINES—WHICH ARE BETTER?

During a lull in one of my workouts recently, I was approached by a well-developed young bodybuilder who wanted to ask "just one question" (which is something no aspiring bodybuilder can possibly do). His one question, of course, led to a lengthy catechism, but I didn't mind as his queries were intelligent and thought-provoking. As we continued our conversation, my interrogator told me he had attended the seminars of practically every top bodybuilder in the world back home in Toronto, Canada. He claimed that even though he did pick up some valuable practical information from a couple of champions, in most cases he left the seminars disappointed. Often contradictory information was dispensed and sometimes even misinformation.

"Like what?" I asked.

"Why sure, Mike, that's easy," he shot back. "There are so many. Just recently one of the greatest bodybuilders of all time held a seminar in our gym and said something to the effect that to create definition in the frontal thighs you shouldn't perform squats, as they ruin definition, and that thigh extensions were best."

"Okay, he was wrong," I replied. "Did you call him on it?"

"Yeah, I told him that there was no such thing as a definition exercise or a bulk exercise. I said that because squats activate more muscles, they burn more calories than thigh extensions and will therefore enhance definition faster."

"What did the champ say then?" I asked.

"Before he could respond, someone in the audience yelled that I was crazy and wanted to know how many titles I had won. The champ then pointed out that he had many more years' experience than me and was obviously more successful. I realized that his seminar was not intended as an open exchange of ideas but a monologue by an egomaniac, so I shut up."

I told the young bodybuilder that he had done well in questioning the champ, but that it was probably best not to push the point, and I resumed my workout. However, the attitude typified by the young bodybuilder is one that's becoming increasingly prevalent among strength athletes all over the world. Everywhere truth-seekers are taking a hard critical look at traditional training and dietary practices. No longer do they automatically swallow the advice of a top champ. No longer will they passively bow to the decree "Thou shalt!" They want a reason, a rationale, some supportive facts—they want to know "Why?" Some bodybuilding traditionalists are growing increasingly alarmed as they witness their rumpus-room picture of bodybuilding systematically slashed by the sports medical specialists, exercise physiologists, nutritionists, and aspiring bodybuilders.

It's no small wonder that the young, questioning bodybuilder of today is often confused by the welter of conflicting opinions regarding sets, reps, how often to train, and which system to use. For years now the different magazines have been teeming with articles that proffer contradictory opinions on precisely what is the best way to train. Now adding to the bodybuilder's dilemma is the raging controversy between the advocates of free weights and those who sing the praises of the machine.

Although there has been a massive proliferation of exercise machines on the market—Nautilus, Bowflex, Universal, Hammer Strength, Bodymasters, and Cybex to mention some of the more prominent ones—the epicenter of the storm for years has been Nautilus, the first (perhaps the only) machine manufacturer that actually conducted its own large-scale research in sports medicine and exercise physiology, and turned out reams of copy on its results, much of which ran contrary to the prevailing worldview. Another reason Nautilus was the subject of so much controversy probably had to do with its rise as the leading manufacturer of exercise equipment (with sales in 1981—the year in which it received the most heat from the bodybuilding establishment—reportedly in the neighborhood of $350 million).

It's important for bodybuilders struggling to arrive at some understanding of the controversy to realize that the prejudice encountered among the people involved is a strange one indeed, but a very real one that must be considered. A biased selection and distorted representation of statistics are often claimed as evidence, "proving" points that are often the opposite of the truth. Most of what has been written about the various modes of training comes from the equipment manufacturers themselves, which thus makes it suspect.

I'm not really interested in proving anyone right or wrong. Such an approach would point to a bias on my part, making my viewpoint just as suspect. What I am interested in is an objective look at the facts as they exist so that the bodybuilder can make his own enlightened decision as to which mode works best.

A bodybuilder will reach a reasonable conclusion only if he can examine the various points of controversy with adequate information. The following discussion should help him develop his own conclusions.

FREE WEIGHTS—PROS AND CONS

Before Alan Calvert invented the plate-loading barbell around the turn of the century, the bodybuilder and strength athletes as we know them today didn't exist. It is obvious that the barbell produced muscular size that was impossible before its appearance. Compared to anything that came before it, the barbell was a

Dumbbells offer the advantage of being able to train your muscles unilaterally (one arm at a time); this allows for a stronger contractile impulse to reach the muscles from the brain.

miracle implement. The fact that the barbell is a productive tool—when used properly—cannot be denied as the vast majority of today's champion bodybuilders and strength athletes were literally weaned on it. This does not alter the fact that the barbell still has certain shortcomings.

For a proper understanding of the shortcomings of a barbell we must take a look at the basic underlying effective training methodology. While our various bodyparts move in a rotary fashion about an axis, most conventional free weight equipment provides only straight-line, or unidirectional resistance. This accounts for the fact that in most exercises the weight feels heavier in some positions than in others, and very rarely is there any resistance at all in the peak or fully contracted position, the only position where 100 percent of the individual muscle fibers can be activated.

The curl, for example, a movement that is rotational through a range of some 160 degrees, provides effective resistance only through a very small area of the curl's entire range of motion. Only at that point in the curl where the forearms are perfectly parallel to the ground, where gravity is pulling the weight straight down and you are pulling it straight up, is the resistance direct. Once the weight passes through that point, the effective resistance falls off and the weight feels light, with little or no resistance in the contracted position.

Conventional free-weight exercises such as overhead barbell presses or the clean and jerk exercise provide little effective resistance when the elbows are locked out.

In those barbell exercises where you can lock out and hold the weight in the peak contracted position, there is no resistance to force contraction. This is a major drawback of the barbell since, again, the contracted position is so important for growth stimulation. Examples of barbell exercises where lockouts occur are squats, leg presses, presses of any sort, and curls. In the lockout all effective resistance has been removed from the muscle and is being supported by the bones, which are in a straight-line position. When this happens, the muscles can relax and since there is no resistance for them to fight against, there is limited growth stimulation.

The existence of a sticking point—that point in an exercise where the resistance is heavier than at other points—makes it clear that the muscles are being worked harder in some positions than others. A lockout, or a position where the weight can be supported with little or no muscular involvement, points to the fact that the muscles are not being worked at all. All this demonstrates that barbell exercises provide resistance for the muscles only in their weakest positions and add little or no resistance in their strongest positions. Since

The dumbbell lateral raise is an example of a free-weight exercise that provides resistance in the peak or fully contracted position.

everyone is aware that resistance and intensity are the factors that cause growth stimulation, it should be perfectly obvious that where no resistance occurs there can be little growth stimulation—and in most barbell exercises that is just the situation we find in the peak contracted position of the muscles. There are exercises that are productive in spite of these limiting factors, though not nearly as effective as they would be without such limitations.

EXERCISE MACHINES— PROS AND CONS

If an exercise machine does not provide advantages that more than compensate for its inherent disadvantages, then you're better off sticking to free weights. And considering the inherent disadvantages of most exercise machines, one would have to conclude that most of them—though not necessarily all—are actually less productive than the barbell. Following are some of the oft-cited advantages and disadvantages of the exercise machine.

Mechanical Specificity, or Guided Resistance

The one disadvantage inherent in all exercise machines without exception is this factor of guided resistance. The resistance provided by

The triceps pushdown machine was a staple of Mike Mentzer's training during his competitive days.

exercise machines is limited to a single track of movement, unlike the barbell, which allows freedom of movement in any direction. Because certain barbell exercises can approximate the mechanics of certain movements found in different athletic events such as shot putting and jump-related activities, they can be used to enhance performance in those events. Bodybuilders trying to work specific areas of a muscle can do so with barbells by altering the angle of resistance. Machines do not allow this because of the restricted single track of movement.

Reverse Geometry

As mentioned previously, barbells provide resistance in only one direction—down vertically, as a result of gravity. By using pulleys, resistance can be redirected in any direction desired. But even in such cases the resistance is

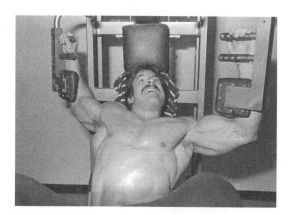

The Nautilus flye machine, as well as popular pec deck machines, allow the pectoral muscles to fulfill their primary function to draw the arm across the midline of the body. Some of the more advanced machines also allow for unilateral training.

still in only one direction, or unidirectional. What you end up with is an exercise almost identical to a barbell exercise and in some cases less effective than a barbell exercise. Machines that work muscles that cannot be worked by a barbell are certainly justified. Examples of worthwhile applications of redirected barbell exercises are the lat machine and the leg press machine.

Machines that work on the leverage principle are probably the least productive, least efficient of all. Although levers are not as subject to breakdown from wear as cables are, they do suffer from greatly reduced function. The machines that use levers apply resistance opposite the strength curve of most muscles; in most cases there is way too much resistance in the extended or weakest position, making it almost impossible to get the weight started, and too little in the mid-range and contracted positions, making the remainder of the movement too easy, with little or no effective resistance.

The so-called variable resistance machines—Nautilus being the best known—have attempted to increase available resistance throughout the entire range of motion in an attempt to overcome the shortcomings of the barbell. Nautilus has provided for automatically variable resistance that corresponds to the strength curve of the muscle through its full range of motion by means of an offset cam. And while the Nautilus cam may not provide the perfectly balanced resistance that the manufacturer claims, it is highly probable that it comes closer to being more perfectly balanced than the unidirectional resistance provided by barbells and the resistance of reverse geometry provided by some of the other machines on the market.

Power Output

It has been suggested that machines do not permit very rapid movements and therefore do not permit the development of power, which is important to the bodybuilder trying to become more massive. It is true that Nautilus has gone on record repeatedly stating that all exercise movements should be performed deliberately and under control so as to obviate the very real possibility that momentum might aid in completing the movement and thus reduce power output and intensity, not to mention that deliberate motion makes any exercise safer. What is not true is that the movements cannot be performed rapidly. The fact is that, although such a practice is both unproductive and unsafe, rapid movements can be performed on machines.

Direct Exercise

I have already mentioned the fact that direct resistance is not provided by barbells because they provide only straight-line, or unidirectional, resistance to bodyparts that move in a rotary fashion and are thus constantly changing the direction in which they move. Because of this, the weight will feel heavier in some positions and lighter in others, often with no resistance at all in the important peak contracted position. As far as I know, Nautilus and Hammer Strength are the only machine manufacturers that have endeavored to overcome this shortcoming by providing resistance that is directly opposed to the movement, or 180 degrees out of phase with the movement. Whether or not they succeeded is debatable. The preceding considers only one of the two distinct meanings of the word *direct* in its application to exercise. Direct in the other sense means the resistance must be applied against the prime mover, or the bodypart moved by the involved muscles. In this sense Nautilus has provided direct exercise by designing machines that place the source of resistance against the prime mover. In the case of the latissimus, Nautilus with their pullover machine has applied the resistance against the prime mover, the upper arm, instead of against the forearm and hand as is the case with all other conventional machine or free-weight exercise. As explained in the preceding chapter regarding the pre-exhaust principle, any lat exercise that applies resistance to the forearms creates a weak link owing to a proportionate lack of strength in the upper arms. The lats

"In the case of the latissimus, Nautilus with their pullover machine has applied the resistance against the prime mover, the upper arm, instead of against the forearm and hand as is the case with all other conventional machine or free-weight exercise." Mentzer works his lats on the Nautilus behind neck machine.

never reach a point of true muscular failure because the upper arms fail first.

A SYNTHESIS

Individuals who have spent enormous amounts of time, energy, and money selling a particular idea or product often become so intent on seeing their creation accepted by others that they tend to lose their objectivity. This blindness has afflicted the inventors, manufacturers, and purveyors of free weights and machines and has even affected the philosophies (if you

can call them that) behind each. The stakes are no longer just commercial/financial, but in some manner intellectual/philosophical.

The advocates of free weights point to the fact that the vast majority of bodybuilding and strength athletes have trained on free weights. Their stand is not entirely valid since so have all the failures. Those who push machines are just as blind in their exaggerated claims that these devices will produce results unheard of with free weights. The tactics used by each side in selling its products have focused so much on the relatively small differences contained in each that they've lost sight of the fundamental similarity in the two. Free weights and machines are both progressive-resistance tools that must adhere to the basic high-intensity principles of progression and intensity if they are to work for anyone. Machines are not that different from free weights. No matter which the bodybuilder decides to use, he must move a certain resistance a certain distance in a certain time. Whether he uses free weights, machines, or cinder blocks, the individual will get larger and stronger only by progressively increasing the level of resistance.

Recognizing that free weights and machines each have their strengths and weaknesses, would it not be more rational to discover the strong points of each and fuse them than continue to focus on their shortcomings? As bodybuilding is my vocation, I have investigated the strengths and weaknesses of free weights and machines as objectively as possible. My ongoing research has led me to formulate a tentative conclusion on how the bodybuilder can best utilize the two modes in a combination that is based on an application of the high-intensity principles of adaptation and specificity, according to the needs, respectively, of the beginning, intermediate, and advanced bodybuilder.

The beginner, for instance, must develop neuromuscular coordination, overall strength, and conditioning, along with an appreciation of the kinesthetic pleasure to be derived from weight training. While Universal, Nautilus, Hammer Strength, and the other machines can develop overall strength and improve conditioning, they don't allow the freedom of move-

"The barbell clean and press brings into play practically every muscle of the body in one unified coordinated action, thereby developing great overall power and neuromuscular control."—Mike Mentzer

ment required to work the mass of muscles in a single motion or develop the base of power and neuromuscular coordination. The beginner should not be concerned with developing a highly refined, rococo appearance. A solid foundation must be built first. Barbells and free weights are better suited for this as more muscles under greater resistance can be brought into play. The guided resistance provided by machines is too restrictive and works the muscles more in an isolation manner, though a few do work some accessory muscles. An example is the barbell clean and press, which brings into play practically every muscle of the body in one unified coordinated action, thereby developing great overall power and neuromuscular control.

This kind of compound movement performed with a barbell is much better for creating overall mass and power than the isolation movements provided by most machines. When I was a youngster of about 16 and was stuck at 200 pounds in the military press, I was able to press 210 or sometimes even 215 with the help of a slight shove from my traps, hips, and waist. Getting the heavier weight overhead and then lowering it under control brought in more muscle fibers and developed my confidence. Doing strict presses would have kept me stuck at the same weight for weeks.

The freedom of movement allowed by free weights can be used to teach the beginning bodybuilder to marshal his strength in a specific area and release it explosively for the handling of heavier weights. Free weights also provide the psychological satisfaction gained in seeing and feeling a heavier weight than usual and in overcoming an obstacle. This visual feedback is the fuel that motivates the bodybuilder to continue. Most machines don't provide this important feedback and the less resolute beginner can become bored and quit.

As the beginner continues to train regularly, using the basic exercises, he develops a solid foundation of power, mass, and familiarity with his functional capacities.

The intermediate bodybuilder—one who has been engaged in regular training with free weights for upwards of six months to a year—should begin focusing her attention on the development of individual bodyparts and controlling them with her will as a means of refining their appearance. At this point, the bodybuilder can also focus on her weak points as not all bodyparts grow evenly—specialization at this time is important for maintaining

balance and symmetry. The intermediate would do well to use machines about 25 percent of the time in her training at this point.

The advanced (i.e., competitive) bodybuilder zooming in for a contest can use all types of equipment, including machines, cables, and free weights. The machine exercises along with all forms of dipping and chinning will be useful in helping him further chisel his muscles and sharpen his definition besides overcoming his weak points. In this way he can still use the free weights for chiseling and maintaining mass as well as rely on the machines for further refinement and balance. The more advanced bodybuilder is still well advised to train predominantly in the off-season with free weights in his continuing quest for mass. Machines are especially great as adjuncts during the pre-contest phase for that ultimate look of refinement.

In closing I'd like to emphasize that while free weights and machines are capable of working wonders in their respective ways, neither is magic, and only total dedication and sustained effort over a period of time can produce optimal results. So, as the bodybuilder grows in experience, he may formulate his own mode of training based on what he decides best suits his needs at any given time. Whatever method of training you decide on, I hope your decision is made after you have objectively assessed the available information.

Competitive bodybuilders should make use of both machines and free weights in their training.

Part IV

PUTTING THEORY INTO PRACTICE

"The biochemical changes that result in muscular growth are essentially the same in all individuals."
—Mike Mentzer

Chapter 13

THE IDEAL (PRINCIPLED) WORKOUT

The principles elucidated in the preceding chapters apply to every bodybuilder—and to every single human being. Why? If the laws of science were not immutable, if they were subject to arbitrary change, then science itself could not exist as a viable discipline. If, for example, the laws of physics were not immutable, we could not send men to the moon and bring them back to earth again. If the laws of physiology didn't apply to everyone, the science of medicine could not exist. The fact that the results of experiments on specific individuals can be applied to the general populace makes medicine a viable science.

The biochemical changes that result in muscular growth are essentially the same in all individuals. And the type of stimulation required to induce those specific biochemical changes is the same for the entire species. Though it is true that no two individuals are identical, as there will always be variations in anatomical structure and stress tolerance, for example, those variations fall within a limited range. Where one bodybuilder may find that a particular exercise causes him to respond bet-

The training routine listed in this chapter will induce maximum growth stimulation while utilizing a minimum of the body's recuperative resources.

ter than might another, due to a structural advantage he possesses, both individuals still possess limited physical resources, and both will better stimulate the biochemical changes leading to muscle growth if they engage in high-intensity training.

For a training routine to be productive it must, of course, stimulate muscular growth. A routine that stimulates growth must also allow that growth to take place, having been stimulated. This means that the routine must not be so long that it causes the body to deplete its recuperative capacity in an attempt to cope with the exhaustive effects of the exercise.

An ideal routine, then, would:

1. Induce maximum possible growth stimulation.
2. Use up a minimum of the body's recuperative capacities.

With the following high-intensity training program, these two requirements of an ideal routine have been fulfilled. We know by now that high intensity of effort is an absolute requirement for stimulating rapid increases in size and strength, and that since high-intensity training must be of short duration it will deplete relatively little of the body's resources. Some of the principles that are incorporated in this workout routine are generally known, while others (such as the functions of muscular structures—an application of the principles of identity and specificity) are somewhat obscure. It is important that each reader develop an understanding of all of these principles because they form the logical basis of the high-intensity training system.

Because of the stressful nature of high-intensity training, you should not hurry through these workouts at first. Spend the first couple of weeks learning the exercises and making proper weight selections. In time you will adapt to the higher stress levels and will be able to speed up the pace. It may take as long as 30 minutes to complete the routines at first, but the time required will gradually diminish until it only takes 10 to 12 minutes to do the routines. This reduction in workout time over a period is imperative because intensity, if you recall, is related to the time it takes to complete a given amount of work. You must make unceasing efforts towards reducing workout time; just don't be in such a hurry that you exceed your physiological limits, lest you end up on the gym floor in a state of shock. Rest four to seven days after performing each of these workouts.

WORKOUT ONE: CHEST AND BACK

All of the major muscle groups possess certain attributes that make them pleasing to the eye. Those attributes that seem to arrest the viewer's attention the most concern the complexity and multiformity of design. Consider, for example, the myriad individual muscles that go to form the back, which is the largest muscle area of the torso and, in my opinion,

the most beautiful. The most complex muscular formation in the back is the trapezius, also known as the traps, which arises from the base of the skull and spreads out in a thick sheath to cover the shoulder blades and upper back and converges to a point in the middle of the back along the spine. Then there is the latissimus dorsi, or lats, which is simpler in design than the trapezius, but is bulkier and gives breadth to the back. As popular as the traps and lats are to most bodybuilders, it is actually the smaller,

more intricate muscles of the upper back that are responsible for the back's interesting detail. How many are familiar with the teres, the rhomboideus, and the infraspinatus? These are the little muscles that are so visible in a highly developed cut-up back and which really catch the audience's attention.

The pectorals are comprised of a pectoral major and minor, which appear together as a single structure with no interesting detail when they are in a relaxed state. Upon being flexed, however, the pecs will lift and divide into their two major portions, the major and minor, and splinter into thousands of fibrous striations across their entire width. It is this property of the pecs that causes them to appear as spectacular sunbursts of radiating striations that has made the most muscular or "crab" pose so popular with the aficionados.

Certainly no serious bodybuilder with competitive aspirations would neglect the development of the torso. Where many young bodybuilders do err, however, is in neglecting to learn the anatomy of these structures. Ignorance of the fact that the pecs have an upper portion and a lower portion has led many to neglect developing one or the other of the two portions—usually the upper—resulting in an imbalanced disproportionate development. Many think of the back as merely the lats. Those who train just the lats and never seriously work the traps and small muscles of the upper inner back may develop breadth but will lack the very important density and depth of development that makes the back such an interesting spectacle to behold. Of course, to lack development anywhere in these key areas of the torso won't help in competition either.

Forming the core of the body, the judges' gaze will always go to the torso first.

The workout below is designed to work the major muscles of the torso as well as the smaller, more intricate ones. The exercises that are outlined are familiar standards that everyone except the rank beginner will know. The pointers that are included with each exercise should prove helpful, but more important is the proper implementation of the principles that form the basis of the high-intensity training system of bodybuilding. The success you have with this routine will be contingent not so much on the exercises you employ as on the strict adherence to the scientific principles of effective muscle building. (Please note that a comprehensive list of workout points will follow the presentation of the three workouts.)

Chest Exercise 1: Dumbbell Flyes

This is a great exercise for isolating the pecs and preserving the strength of the triceps for the incline press that is to follow immediately.

With the dumbbells together over the face, lower them to the sides with the elbows pulled back and out to the sides. Lower to a position

Dumbbell flyes can be performed on either a flat bench or slight incline bench.

just below the plane of the torso, and no further, or you might injure the shoulder. Keeping the angle in the elbows consistent throughout the raising of the weight back to the top will stress the pecs, preserve the triceps strength, and reduce strain on the connective tissue in the crook of the elbow. It doesn't matter if the weights touch at the top, since at that point there is no resistance to fight against anyway. Move immediately upon completion of one set of 6 to 10 repetitions in this exercise (to the point of muscular failure) to the next exercise.

Chest Exercise 2: Incline Presses

This is the compound exercise that will call into play the fresh strength of the triceps to aid in working the pecs, which were pre-fatigued by the flyes. Since the pecs will be exhausted from the flyes, you won't be able to use as much weight in this exercise as usual.

With a shoulder-width grip, lower the bar to the neck slowly, with the elbows pointed directly out to the side. It is the position of the elbows, more than the hand spacing, that places the greatest stress on the pecs. A common training mistake is to do this exercise with a wide hand spacing with the idea that this stretches the pecs more. Actually, just the opposite is true. A closer hand spacing causes the pecs to stretch and work over a greater range of motion. As proof, witness how little the humerus, or upper arm, which is the insertion point for the pecs, moves in a wide-grip incline or regular bench press. Since the function of the pecs is to bring the upper arm into and across the midline of the torso, the elbows must be held out to the sides so the pecs can perform their function in this exercise. Perform one set of 1 to 3 repetitions until failure.

Back Exercise 1: Straight-Arm Lat Machine Pulldowns

This is one of the few exercises that can be done for the lats without involving the biceps. This will be the isolation exercise used in the isolation/compound cycle.

The lat machine bar should be over your head and slightly in front of you so that you'll

Incline presses are the compound movement to carry your pecs past a point of positive muscular failure.

have to pull it in towards your body. With a shoulder-width grip pull the arms into the thighs, keeping them almost perfectly straight. The idea is to save the strength of your biceps, so it is imperative that you keep the arms straight. Hold the bar at thigh level for a distinct pause before allowing the bar to return slowly to the top overhead position. Watch how sore your abs and serratus get from this great exercise, in addition to the lats. Move immediately upon completion of one set of 6 to 10

Straight-arm lat machine pulldowns are an effective isolation movement for the lats.

Palms-up pulldowns allow your lats to continue to contract beyond a point of positive failure by bringing the fresh biceps into play to aid in making the movement.

repetitions (to the point of muscular failure) to the next exercise.

Back Exercise 2: Palms-Up Pulldowns

With the same lat machine used in the straight-arm pulldown, change your grip immediately upon adding weight and continue with the palms-up (underhand) pulldowns. The underhand grip is used because it places the biceps into their strongest position. Most bodybuilders use the palms-down overhead grip that places the biceps in a weak position, limiting the degree to which you can work your back. Another mistake made by bodybuilders is using the wide grip in the pulldown and in

chinning movements. Rather than stretch the lats—which is the logic behind using the wide grip—the wide grip actually reduces the stretch, or the range of motion over which the lats contract. Place your upper arm up by your head and feel how much the lats are stretched, and then lower it to the side, as in a wide grip position, and you'll see that the stretch is greatly diminished. Pull the bar from overhead into the chest around the nipple area, hold for a pause, and return slowly to the top. Perform one set of 6 to 10 repetitions until failure.

Back Exercise 3: Deadlifts

This is the most stressful exercise of the program—along with squats—for it involves the most muscles. The considerable stresses involved make the deadlift the most productive exercise of all. The best way to visualize the proper performance of the deadlift is to imagine it as a combination of a deep knee bend and toe touch. Start with the barbell rolled back flush against the shins, then grasp it with a slightly wider than shoulder-width grip. (You

Deadlifts—Mike Mentzer considered the deadlift to be the best overall body exercise in existence because it taxed virtually every muscle in the body, thereby stimulating tremendous overall muscle growth.

Mentzer's back development was awesome to behold—note the tremendous thickness of his erector spinae muscles in the lower back.

can use a regular grip, or if the weight is really heavy, use an "over/under" grip, in which one palm faces forward and the other backward, for greater strength.) Bend down in such a manner that your shoulders are higher than your hips (or buttocks) and, most importantly, keep your back flat and your head up. With arms perfectly straight and no jerking or pulling, stand up with the bar until your body is perpendicular to the ground (there is no good reason to arch backwards at the top). Upon reaching the top, pause briefly, and lower under control to the floor in the same manner as you lifted—back flat and head up. Once the barbell is on the floor, reassume the proper form, reset psychologically, take a deep breath, and repeat. This exercise works every muscle on the back side of the body from the calves to the leg biceps, the gluteus, hips, spinal erectors, latissimus, deltoids, arms—really every muscle of the body. (If I could only choose one exercise, it would be deadlifts because, again, it is the most intense, or demanding, and therefore the most productive. It is very stimulating not just for the muscles, but for all of the physio-

logical subsystems, including the cardiovascular system.) Perform one set of 6 to 10 repetitions until failure.

Rest four to seven days before performing the next workout.

WORKOUT TWO: LEGS AND ABDOMINALS

Harmony and balance are the touchstones of a truly great physique. The higher ranks of the bodybuilding world abound with classically chiseled chests, mind-blowing biceps, barn door–wide backs, and washboard abdominals,

"The rope."

inside of the thigh writhing and twisting like some giant serpent. From there on it's downhill and you've got them eating out of your hand.

I was never one to resist working the legs. From the time I took up bodybuilding, leg work actually came first. Having played football and a little track and field, it seemed the smart thing to do. The long-term benefits were the most rewarding. The foundation I laid with those early squat workouts contributed, I believe, to my ability to develop muscle at a rapid rate later on, when I wanted it the most.

Don't neglect those leg workouts thinking you'll make up for it later on. The imbalance that will result could be ruinous in that you may never overcome it. Getting the legs to respond will have a very beneficial effect on the rest of the body. When growth is stimulated in any muscle, then growth is also stimulated, though to a lesser degree, in the rest of the body. This indirect effect seems to be proportional to the size of the muscle being stimulated. Since the legs are the biggest muscles in the body, their stimulation will have the greatest effect of stimulating growth in the rest of the body.

The group of muscles that form the leg is so large that the exercises to work the legs are especially taxing. The drain that hard leg work places on the body's reserves is so great that special caution must be taken when we work them. The possibility of overtraining looms ever present when we do leg work, so the absolute minimum amount of exercise must be done that will still stimulate growth. The leg routine offered in this workout is ideal. The exercises are performed sequentially and in such a manner that maximum growth stimulation is achieved with only a minimum drain placed upon the body's reserves.

Training the Calves

The calf has come to be known as the stubborn muscle. Because of all the exercise the calves receive in our daily routine, as the rationale goes, such as walking, climbing, running, the calves are especially tough and stubborn. That may be true; I really don't know. But I do

but the paucity of great leg development within the competing ranks is downright appalling. Only those whose legs have reached parity with their upper bodies can ever hope to take the giant step into the category of elite bodybuilder.

Sure, leg work can be a real bitch. But, man, is it worth it when you know you've got some pretty mean pins down there, and the audience is chanting for you to give them one of your special leg shots. After a whole evening of mediocre legs parading by, the audience is primed and waiting for something outrageous. The first pose you give them is "the rope," which displays the sartorius muscle on the

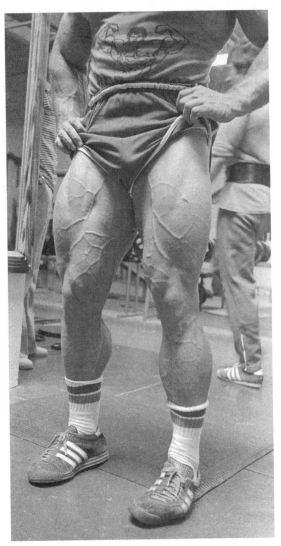

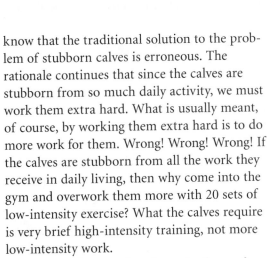

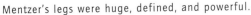

Mentzer's legs were huge, defined, and powerful.

know that the traditional solution to the problem of stubborn calves is erroneous. The rationale continues that since the calves are stubborn from so much daily activity, we must work them extra hard. What is usually meant, of course, by working them extra hard is to do more work for them. Wrong! Wrong! Wrong! If the calves are stubborn from all the work they receive in daily living, then why come into the gym and overwork them more with 20 sets of low-intensity exercise? What the calves require is very brief high-intensity training, not more low-intensity work.

Walking is a very low-intensity form of activity, which is why we can do so much of it.

To try to build stubborn calves with high-rep sets of daily workouts is like trying to put out a fire with kerosene. The calves must be worked no more than once a week with heavy weights over a full range of movement and carried to a point of failure where the weight can't possibly be budged no matter how hard you try. How many sets? One.

Training the Abdominals

There seems to have been a tendency in some of the heavier top bodybuilders over the years to neglect the abdominals. It was believed, and long seemed to be true, that the really large

At a body weight of 215 pounds, Mentzer's abdominals were defined and deeply chiseled.

importance for today's competitors to pay particular attention to the abdominal region.

I fully realize that the prevailing wisdom has most bodybuilders performing countless low-intensity sets and reps so as not to over-develop the abdominals. It seems silly to me that bodybuilders should want to develop large arms, chests, legs, backs, and leave the abs puny. What could be more ridiculous and incongruous than a thickly developed body-builder of 200 pounds who has the abdominal development of a 160-pound man! Thick, proportionately developed rectus abdominus (frontal abs) set off a well-developed physique and will not thicken or broaden one's waist. The breadth of your abdominal region is dictated primarily by your pelvic bone width, which is inherited and therefore not subject to alteration. I always train my abs in high-intensity fashion just like my other bodyparts because, yes, high-intensity training will make your abs thicker, which should be your goal. The abdominals are skeletal muscles—just like the biceps and calves—and therefore their training requirement is no different from these other muscle groups. The abdominals don't require volume training but high-intensity training, which, as we know, must be intense, brief, and infrequent. Training your muscles in this manner will result in superb abdominal development that, when combined with a reduced calorie diet to strip off excess bodyfat, will cause your abs to stand out in bold relief.

Leg Exercise 1: Leg Extensions

This exercise is very valuable in that it focuses the stress almost entirely on the frontal thigh muscles. This isolation of those muscles is important because the strength of the adjacent muscle groups like adductors on the inside of the thighs and the buttocks is preserved for the second exercise to follow, leg presses. When performing exercises such as leg presses or squats, the weaker adjacent muscle groups such as the hips, lower back, or buttocks give out first. Doing the leg extensions first makes use of the pre-exhaust principle so that when we go immediately to the second exercise, the leg presses, the adjacent muscle groups will have a

super-developed champs could get by on mass alone with no one noticing their lack of sharp abdominal delineation.

That may have been the case up until now, but these days with competition the way it is a bodybuilder has to be refined as well as massive in appearance. That means he's got to have every muscle group thoroughly chiseled with absolutely no trace of fatty tissue blurring the effect. This is especially true of the midsection since it is the focal point of the physique. The eyes tend to fall on the midsection first before traveling elsewhere, so it is of paramount

Leg extensions—be sure to pause in the fully contracted position before lowering the resistance.

Leg Exercise 2: Leg Presses

This exercise is particularly effective in stimulating growth because of the heavier weights that can be employed. At one time I had trouble developing mass in my vastus lateralis, or the outer sweep, until I got into some serious leg pressing. I eventually got to the point where I could do eight reps with 1,100 pounds, and the vastus problem ended.

It is essential that you position yourself properly under the leg press, or the great downward pressure might injure your lower back. I am most comfortable with my buttocks positioned slightly forward of the leg press. I seem to be stronger and more stable that way. To begin this exercise, lie on your back with your feet solidly planted on a foot board. Place your feet shoulder-width or slightly wider than shoulder-width on the foot board and point them out a bit. Your hips should be placed so

temporary strength advantage and the thigh muscles can go to a point of failure without the weaker adjacent muscles giving out first.

Using a special machine designed for this exercise, sit firmly in the seat with your back against the pad, positioned so that your lower legs hang freely, with the back of the knees at the edge of the seat pad. Adjust the machine or your position so that the area just slightly above the front of the ankles makes contact with the pads of the movement arm. While grasping the handles lightly to stabilize yourself, move against the ankle pads evenly and deliberately so that the lower legs move out and up until your knees are locked and you're in the straight-legged position. Pause for two seconds, and lower under control. This is the perfect exercise for isolating and working the quadriceps on the front of the thighs. Perform one set of 12 to 20 repetitions until failure and then immediately perform the next exercise.

Leg presses can be done either vertically, as shown in this photo, or on a special 45-degree machine, depending upon what equipment is available to you.

you feel stable while lowering your legs. Bend your legs (lowering your thighs) until they almost hit the chest, but no lower. Going any lower will hyperextend the lower back muscles and make them prone to injury. This can and will happen with any deviation from strict, controlled exercise performance. For safety, particularly when the weights start really getting heavy, you should fold your arms over your chest to prevent severe compression of the thorax when the weight descends. You can also keep your hands on your upper thighs throughout the movement so that if you lapse, or lose control, you can use the strength of your arms to assist in getting the weight back to the top where you can rack the weight and safely get out of the machine. Not only does this exercise work the quadriceps, or frontal thighs, it works the gracilis and semitendonosis on the inside of the upper leg and the back of the legs (the biceps femoris) as well. Perform one set of 12 to 20 repetitions until failure.

Calf Exercise 1: Standing Calf Raises

The only part of the legs left to work is the lower legs, the calves, or gastrocnemius. If training in a commercial gym, use a standing calf machine if one is available. Step up under the shoulder pads and place the balls of your feet onto the cross board, which is several inches off the ground. With your body perfectly straight and knees absolutely locked, raise up on the balls of your feet as high as you can go. This is important as it makes for a full, high-intensity contraction, which is necessary for full stimulation of the muscle. As I tell my own personal training clients: "Try to get to the tip top of your toes, like a ballet dancer. I know you can't, but try it!" Having achieved that position, hold it for two to three seconds, then lower under control. Perform one set of 12 to 20 repetitions until failure.

Abdominal Exercise 1: Sit-Ups

Sit-ups can be done on any of the innumerable new machines available for abdominal training in most health clubs. At home they can be done

Standing calf raises—rise up as high as you can go for a full contraction of the calf muscles.

on a sit-up board or on the floor with your feet held down by a spotter, or by placing them under anything that will stabilize you.

With regular sit-ups, be sure to bend the knees to a 45-degree angle and keep your arms folded across your chest. Performing them in this manner will help remove unnecessary stress from the lower back. Having assumed the proper position, sit up—curl at the waist until your torso is just shy of being perpendicular to the floor, with tension still on the abdominal muscles. When you can do more than 20 reps with your body weight, hold a barbell plate in your folded arms (at the chest) so that you're only able to do 10 to 12 reps. Stay with that new weight until you can do 20. Unlike the other exercises, where more weight can be handled, increase the weight by only five pounds when the upper limit of the prescribed rep range has been reached. Increasing the weight by 10 percent will be impossible with-

Sit-ups can be performed on the floor with your feet tucked under a support such as a barbell, or on a bench that allows you to train them at a slightly different angle.

out special equipment—or until you're handling 50 pounds or more in this exercise.

Rest four to seven days before performing the next workout.

WORKOUT THREE: SHOULDERS AND ARMS

Broad shoulders, more than any other physical trait, might justifiably be termed the mark of a man. Massive arms, a thick chest, muscular legs, or just about all other bodyparts can be concealed by clothing—but never the shoulders. You could wear a burlap sack and still the broad-beam expanse of a really well-developed pair of deltoids would be visible. Of course the actual breadth of the shoulders is contingent

upon the length of the clavicles—the shoulder bones. Since our skeletal formation is genetically predetermined—an inherited trait, that is—there is little we can do to increase the length of our clavicles, or any of our bones for that matter. If nature was stingy and you've inherited only average shoulder width or less, don't despair. While there is nothing you can do to alter the actual length of the clavicles, you can thicken, and even broaden to a degree, the deltoid muscles which cap the shoulders.

Larry Scott, of all the great bodybuilders, probably had the least to work with in terms of bone structure. Possessing a less than average shoulder width, Larry went on to develop a pair of the greatest delts of all time. All three portions of his delts were developed to their maximum, causing them to appear as huge,

The phenomenal size and detail of Mentzer's arms and shoulders is particularly evident in this photo, taken at the 1980 Mr. Olympia contest.

oversized cantaloupes. Despite his skeletal deficiency, Larry became one of the greats, and so can you if you want it badly enough.

The deltoids play a very important part in physique competition, more than some of the body's larger muscles. Viewed from the front, the deltoids are responsible for conveying the impression of width—a criterion of central importance in judging a physique; from the side view the delts convey depth and thickness, a sign of mature development; and from the rear view we witness also width but, more important, here we look for evidence of polish. If the posterior portions of the deltoids are highly developed, they will jut up like twin meaty nodules that provide the back with the third dimension of depth, something you rarely see in the novice physique.

I was blessed with greater than average shoulder width along with a small hip structure, a trait that tends to accentuate the illusion of broad shoulders. I never allowed these natural advantages to lull me into a false sense of security regarding the need for maximally developed deltoid muscles. My muscular ideals were guys like Bill Pearl and Reg Park, whose physiques had that ruggedly masculine look that only thick meaty delts can truly impart. Following the lead of my chosen heroes, Pearl and Park, I emphasized shoulder work at various points in my training career.

The muscles that cap our shoulders derive their name *deltoid* from the fourth letter in the Greek alphabet, *delta*. Our deltoids are comprised of three rather distinct portions—the anterior, lateral, and posterior portions—

which, taken together, form a delta, or triangular shape. Each of the three deltoid heads possesses a function. The frontal or anterior portion is designed to raise the arm to the front of the body upon contraction; the lateral, or middle, head lifts the arm to the side and away from the body; while the posterior portion of the deltoid muscle pulls the arm behind the plane of the torso when it contracts.

When aiming for complete and total development of the deltoid muscle, all three heads must be made to perform their natural function of moving the upper arm in some direction away from the torso. Therefore we will have to perform different exercises in our deltoid workout if we wish for complete development. The exercises that we will have to concentrate on to get at all three heads, will be raises of different sorts—with the exception of the anterior portion of the delts, which receives ample stimulation from the dumbbell flye/incline press pre-exhaust training from workout one. The exercises in this workout are the standing lateral raise to hit the side or lateral head of the delt, and the rear or bent-over lateral raise for the posterior portion of the delt.

Training the Arms

The arms, of all bodyparts, seem to be the most universally admired. Whenever a bodybuilder is asked by the public to show them his muscle, it is usually the biceps they are referring to. The appeal of big muscular arms is especially strong among males. Big arms are a symbol of masculinity to the adolescent male and will thus play a part in determining where he is placed in the pecking order by his peers. Even with top bodybuilders, there is a mystique which seems to shroud those with the outrageously large arms.

I can recall the early stages of my own training career when I measured my progress by how much my arms were growing. More than anything in the world I wanted arms as huge as those of my idol, Bill Pearl. Fortunately, I never made the mistake that so many other young bodybuilders did of neglecting the rest of my body and training just the arms.

Mike Mentzer's massive arms were the result of his intense, brief, and infrequent training principles. No bodybuilder has ever matched his triceps development.

The major bulk of the upper arms is made up of the biceps and triceps. The term *biceps* means "two heads," referring to the fact that the muscle on the front of the upper arm is comprised of two parts, an inner and an outer head. *Triceps*, or "three heads," refers to the larger muscle on the backside of the upper arm being made up of three parts, the inner head, the outer head, and the middle head. In choosing the best exercises for stimulating the biceps and triceps, we must look at the function of these muscles.

Biceps

The majority of bodybuilders believe the only function of the biceps to be the flexion of the forearm; that is, bringing the forearm from an extended position to a flexed one closer to the upper arm. This is actually the secondary function of the biceps. Its primary function is to supinate the hand, or turn the palm up. Before the biceps can fulfill its secondary function of flexing the forearm, its primary function of supinating the hand must be fulfilled first. What this means for the bodybuilder is that the palms must be facing directly up when performing biceps work. In order to achieve this

Balanced development of the biceps and triceps are a must in competition and serve to impart a striking appearance to a physique.

Mentzer hitting a side triceps pose.

position, a straight barbell or dumbbell must be employed. The E-Z curl, or cambered bar, which so many bodybuilders use, is actually counterproductive in working the biceps as it causes the hands to be placed away from the supine towards a prone position. Always use a palms-up grip, then, when working the biceps, and perform the exercise through a full range of motion, from full extension to full contraction. These two bits of information are vital if you want to get the most from your biceps training.

Triceps

The primary function of the triceps is to extend the forearm and its secondary one is to bring the upper arm into the body, having

fulfilled its primary function. There are very few ways of working both functions of the triceps with conventional equipment. The best two exercises for doing that are the triceps pressdown on the lat machine and the dip between parallel bars. These two exercises will be focused on here and should be included in all arm routines. It would be possible to stimulate 100 percent of the biceps and triceps bulk—or any muscle's entire bulk—if we could exercise them with direct resistance over their full range of motion. We would need to employ exercise, in other words, that provided resistance for both functions of the muscle. Since there is no conventional exercise equipment that will do that, we must employ a series of exercises designed to work the muscles' various functions and work them from different angles.

Shoulder Exercise 1:
Dumbbell Lateral Raises

This is by far the best exercise for developing that important lateral head of the deltoid. The only way to broaden the shoulders once you've exited puberty is to develop the lateral head of the delt.

While holding a dumbbell in each hand, rest the bells to the sides of your thighs, palms facing your thighs. With a slight bend in the elbows, raise them from that position until your arms are parallel to the ground. Don't raise them to the front, but laterally, directly up from the side of the body. This is the only delt exercise for which I might recommend a slightly looser style of performance than that described for most exercises. If you don't use a slight thrust in the beginning of this movement just to get the weight started, you won't be able to employ a weight heavy enough to provide the necessary resistance in the top, or contracted, position of the exercise. Do not, however, use a weight that requires a ridiculously sloppy style. With only a very slight jerk keep the weight moving with the work of the muscles and hold it at shoulder level for a distinct pause. If you cannot hold it there, remember, you used momentum instead of muscle to perform the work. From the top, lower slowly, and feel the weight all the way back to the starting position. Negatives can be employed here occasionally, by curling the weight to the shoulder and thrusting it to the sides before lowering under control. Perform one set of 6 to 10 repetitions until failure.

Shoulder Exercise 2:
Bent-Over Dumbbell Laterals

While bending over at the waist with a slight bend in the knees (with the torso parallel to the floor), raise the dumbbells until the arms move as far above the torso as possible, pause, and then lower under control. Do 6 to 10 repetitions.

This is a particularly hard exercise to verbally describe. If you're a neophyte, consider hiring a good trainer for a couple of sessions or

Dumbbell lateral raises—one of the best exercises for developing the side or lateral head of the deltoid muscle complex.

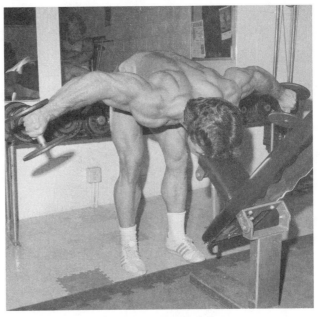

Bent-over dumbbell laterals—hold the fully contracted position for a distinct pause before lowering the dumbbells back to the starting position.

Palms-up pulldowns—one of the greatest biceps developers there is.

Triceps pushdowns—keep the tension on the triceps from beginning to end; don't torque the weight—press it.

until you are confident that you're performing all the exercises properly. (See A Special Note at the end of this chapter.)

Biceps Exercise 1: Palms-Up Pulldowns

While the pulldown is traditionally regarded as a latissimus exercise, it also is a very effective deltoid exercise, and even more so as a biceps exercise. In fact, the close-grip, palms-up pulldown is the best biceps exercise you could do—better than the curl. When performing a curl, whether a Nautilus curl or conventional barbell curl, you work the biceps around a single joint axis, the elbow, and the predominant stress goes into the lower biceps. When performing a close-grip, palms-up pulldown, you are working the biceps around two joint axes, the elbow and the shoulder; thus you are working the biceps muscle more uniformly from both ends. The underhand grip is used because it places the biceps into their strongest position.

Pull the bar from overhead into the chest around the nipple area, hold for a pause, and return slowly to the top. Perform one set of 6 to 10 repetitions until failure.

Triceps Exercise 1: Triceps Pressdowns

I would say that this is one of the most productive triceps exercises you could perform with conventional equipment. Since this exercise causes you to extend the forearms with the upper arms already held in to the body, you work the two functions of the triceps mentioned earlier. This double-barreled action is very important in working all three heads of the triceps.

With a machine similar to the lat pulldown, grasp the bar in front of you with a close grip (hands eight inches apart) with your elbows tucked in at the sides of your waist. There should be no "traveling" of the upper arms away from the tucked-at-the-waist, stable position or the pectorals and latissimus dorsi will come into play. Extend the bar downwards with the body held straight up so that body leverage does not aid in the movement. Lock the elbows firmly at the bottom and pause momentarily before allowing the bar to return slowly to the extended position. Perform 6 to 10 repetitions until failure and then immediately perform the next exercise.

Triceps Exercise 2: Dips

Veteran trainees think of dips as the upper body squat. It is so productive that if I had to choose one exercise for the upper body, it would be dips. (Observe the gymnasts who specialize on the parallel bars; they possess pectorals, deltoids, and triceps similar in development to that of a bodybuilder's.) This exer-

cise will be utilized in the development of the triceps in much the same way that incline presses were used for the pectorals. After carrying a set of pressdowns to a point of momentary failure, a set of dips will follow immediately, so that we can call upon the strength of the pectorals and frontal deltoids to aid the triceps in continuing, even though they are fatigued from the initial isolation exercise. The rest between the two exercises must be literally zero, lest the triceps recover their strength and render the principle of pre-fatigue inoperative.

Dips performed for the triceps should be done with the elbows held in close to the body and the legs held slightly back away from the body, so that you are tipped forward. As with all exercise, perform the dips in a slow and deliber-

Dips—the best exercise there is for building massive triceps.

ate manner, going all the way down at the bottom and locking the elbows at the top. Perform one set of 3 to 5 repetitions until failure.

Rest four to seven days before performing the next workout.

WORKOUT FOUR: LEGS AND ABDOMINALS

Repeat the exercises and protocol as listed in Workout Two.

Rest four to seven days and then repeat the four-workout cycle, beginning with Workout One.

The Workouts in Schematic Form

Workout One: Chest & Back

Chest

Dumbbell flyes for pre-exhaust 1 × 6–10 reps

Incline presses 1 × 1–3 reps

Back

Straight-arm pulldowns for pre-exhaust 1 × 6–10 reps

Palms-up pulldowns 1 × 6–10 reps

Deadlifts 1 × 6–10 reps

Workout Two: Legs & Abs

Legs

Leg extensions for pre-exhaust 1 × 12–20

Leg presses 1 × 12–20

Standing calf raises 1 × 12–20

Abs

Sit-ups 1 × 12–20

Workout Three: Shoulders & Arms

Shoulders

Dumbbell lateral raises 1 × 6–10 reps

Bent-over dumbbell laterals 1 × 6–10 reps

Biceps

Palms-up pulldowns 1 × 6–10 reps

Triceps

Triceps pressdowns for pre-exhaust 1 × 6–10 reps

Dips 1 × 3–5 reps

IMPORTANT POINTS TO KEEP IN MIND

Get a Physical Check-Up

It is very important that before starting this or any training program you consult with your doctor and obtain a thorough check-up. No matter how healthy you may seem, undetected problems could exist. In addition to a full physical, you should have a blood panel done, and men should additionally request a testosterone measure (something not ordinarily included in a general blood test). A normal level of testosterone will be necessary to ensure optimal results from the training program.

When to Exercise

Rather than list specific days on which to exercise, I have enumerated the workouts merely as Workout One, Workout Two, etc., as the particular bodypart workouts won't always fall on the same day. In the beginning you are to exercise once every four days; for example, if Workout One is a Monday, Workout Two would be conducted on a Friday, Workout Three the next Wednesday, and so on. If a scheduling conflict arises, and you can't train on the designated day, wait an extra day. As you gain muscle and strength, increase the time between workouts to six days, seven days, or more.

The time of the day that you train will depend on your daily scheduling and personal preference. Most prefer to train at a time when they feel warmed-up and alert. This can vary greatly; I have clients who train anywhere from five in the morning to early evening. It's up to you. Your schedule and how you feel at particular times of the day will ultimately determine your workout time.

Number of Sets

Perform only one working set of each exercise; that is, one set aside from your warm-ups (which will be explained shortly). If you're having difficulty with the idea of only one set, you are making the common mistake of (mis)applying a principle from economics to exercise. In economics, $1,000 is much better than $1. However, in exercise science more is not necessarily better—in fact, it can be quite the opposite. One set to failure is all that is required to stimulate an increase in strength and size—with no number of lesser sets having the same effect.

Pre-Exhaust Sets

Exercises listed as part of a pre-exhaust cycle should be performed in rapid succession with little or no rest in between. Where a pre-exhaust cycle is not listed, rest as long as you need before proceeding to the next exercise but no longer. As your total fitness improves, you'll be able to move rather quickly through the workout. However, never allow the workout to degenerate into a race against the clock. Depending on your condition, rest as little or as much as necessary before moving to the second exercise listed in the pre-exhaust cycle.

Number of Reps

Perform approximately 6 to 10 reps of the exercises listed, except the following: incline presses and dips, do 3 to 5 (if listed as the second exercise in a pre-exhaust set); abdominals and leg exercises, perform 12 to 20 reps.

Proper Exercise Performance

For best results, perform all exercises in a strict manner. This means taking four seconds to lift the weight, pausing two seconds at the top, and lowering for four seconds. The important thing is that there is no momentum assisting in mov-ing the resistance, with the muscles doing all the work. This helps to maximize the stress on the muscles, which is the goal. Controlled repetitions make for much safer exercise too.

Training to Failure

Many weight trainees fail to achieve their goals due to their reluctance to carry each working set to a point of momentary muscular failure. Contrary to popular belief, the last rep is not the most dangerous, but the safest—but only if proper exercise performance is maintained.

Proper Weight Selection

Select a weight for each exercise that allows for the number of reps advocated and performance in the manner described. Never terminate a set, however, just because the prescribed number of reps has been completed. For example, if you reach 10 reps in the curl, but see that you're capable of doing 13, do 13. You're likely to misjudge the weights for the first workout or two, so be patient. Each time you reach the upper end of the suggested range (for example, achieving 10 reps within the prescribed 6 to 10 rep range), add approximately 10 percent to the weight for your next workout. However, if 6 reps is the minimum suggested and you get only 4 or 5, that's fine. The next workout, you'll likely get 6, 7, or even more reps. If you have joint pains or old injuries, use lighter weights and do higher reps (as many as 20 if necessary). As long as you're reaching failure, an increase will be stimulated.

The Warm-Up

Make sure that you spend some time warming the muscles to be worked. However, it is not necessary to stretch the muscles, perform aerobic work, or engage in any more exercise than is minimally required to limber up and increase the blood flow to the specific muscles you're working that day. Using the deadlift as an example: if you're able to handle 165 pounds for 7 reps on your working set, start your warm-up with 115 pounds for 7 to 10 easy reps to get the blood flowing into the area, and then one more set with 145 for 2 or 3 reps to mentally prepare you for the heavier set to follow.

Where pre-exhaust cycles are listed, start the warm-up with the second exercise. For example, warm up with leg presses in the case of the leg extension/leg press pre-exhaust cycle. This will ensure that you'll have warmed up all the necessary muscles, including the quadriceps for the leg extensions, and enable you to pre-set the leg press weight. If you don't warm up with leg presses—which works multiple muscles simultaneously—and instead start with the leg extension, your auxiliary muscles will be cold and the weight won't be pre-set, making it difficult to move with no rest directly to the leg press station.

Warm-up needs do vary among individuals according to age, existing condition, and of course the temperature of the gym you work out in. Keep in mind too that the first few reps of this high-intensity, low-force program serve as a further warm-up. The guiding principle here is: perform the minimal amount of exercise required to achieve an actual warm-up.

Keeping a Progress Chart

Do not evaluate your workouts by the way you feel, such as whether or not you achieve a pump, get sore, or have a gut feeling that you're doing OK. Feelings as such tell you little or nothing about the success of a workout. In fact, feelings and gut hunches tell us very little about anything. I recall that my good friend John Little (the coauthor of this book) once responded to a muscle magazine editorial touting the superiority of gut feelings over science in this way: "If the editor has a gut feeling, how does he know it isn't gas?"

The only proper way to gauge your workout-to-workout success is by the standard of strength increases. If you're stronger the next workout—up in reps, weight, or both—obviously a positive change took place in the muscle. Record the date of each workout, the exercises, the amount of weight, the number of reps completed properly, and weigh yourself at the beginning of each exercise session. If you

are not increasing the weight used and/or reps completed during each workout, something is wrong—and the number of possible explanations is far from infinite. The following will explain.

Regulating the Volume and Frequency

As you grow stronger over time, the stresses you'll be exposed to will grow progressively greater too. If something isn't done to compensate for the increasing stresses, those stresses will eventually reach a critical point and will constitute overtraining. The first symptom of overtraining will be a slowdown in progress, and if you continue with the same volume and frequency protocol, there will ultimately be a complete cessation of progress. This is known to athletes as a *sticking point*. Compensating for the increasing stresses is rather simple. At the first sign of a slowdown in progress, cease training entirely for two weeks so your body has a chance to fully restore its recovery ability. Upon resumption of training, add an extra day or two of rest between workouts, substitute less demanding exercises, and/or periodically eliminate an exercise from your training sessions. For example, every second or third workout for the chest and back (Day One), eliminate the deadlifts and perform the less demanding shrugs; on shoulder and arm day (Day Three), drop the dips periodically and just do the triceps pressdowns; and on leg day drop the leg extensions and just do the leg presses, calf raises, and sit-ups. While you may be tempted to say that a one-set decrease may not be much, consider that there are relatively few exercises to begin with, so one less set will represent a significant percentage decrease.

Individual exercise stress tolerance is a genetically mediated trait; and like all such traits, it is expressed across a broad continuum; those with greater innate adaptability can train more than those with less. Your best friend will be your progress chart. Lack of progress is almost never due to too little exercise, but too much. If progress is not immediate after a reduction of training frequency, take a two-to-three week layoff, and resume training with even lesser frequency. During periods of physical change—progress—your training requirements must change. Case in point: I have a number of personal clients who are training only once every 10 to 14 days!

A Special Note

Some of you reading this will be training at home, others at a professional health club. If you are unfamiliar with proper exercise performance, you might want to hire a trainer for a couple of sessions to make sure that you're doing the exercises correctly. However, as many trainers use the traditional volume approach to exercise, you should merely ask to be shown how to do the exercises. In fact, you'd do well to take this book with you to the health club and show the trainer precisely which exercises you need to learn. Before hiring one, ask around about the club's trainers (even certified ones) because many don't know much about proper exercise performance, let alone the proper approach to intensity, volume, and frequency. Ask for a high-intensity trainer if one is available; he or she will likely know exactly what you require.

Chapter 14

SUBSTITUTING EXERCISES

The exercises listed in the previous chapter were chosen for a specific reason. This doesn't mean, however, that they can't be substituted with others periodically. If you have problems performing the exercises as listed, or do not have access to the equipment indicated, you can substitute them with the following exercises. The key is not so much the exercises you perform as that you remain true to the basic principles of high-intensity training.

ALTERNATE EXERCISES FOR WORKOUT ONE: CHEST AND BACK

Alternate Isolation Exercises for the Chest

These are referred to as isolation exercises since they almost exclusively work the pectorals (chest muscles) and require little involvement of the shoulders or triceps. (In contrast, the bench press, also intended to work the pecs, necessitates heavy involvement of the shoulders and triceps.) These exercises are performed

with either cable handles and pulleys or the movement arms of a pec deck machine.

Cable Crossovers

To perform cable crossovers, stand between two high pulleys. Take hold of the handles at

Cable crossovers can be performed either bilaterally or unilaterally.

The pec deck is the only exercise that allows for a full contraction of the pectoral muscles in the peak contraction position, thus making it the best solitary chest exercise.

the end of each cable, bending your elbows 20 to 30 degrees, and start each exercise in the back position where the elbows are slightly behind the plane of the torso. Move against the resistance slowly until both hands have been drawn down and across the midline of your torso. Pause in this fully contracted position, then lower under control. Perform one set of 6 to 10 repetitions until failure.

Pec Deck

To utilize the pec deck, sit down inside the machine and position your lower arms perpendicular to the floor with your forearms flat against the movement pads. Push evenly against both pads at once, ending the rep when the movement arms meet in the middle. Pause in the contracted position, then perform the negative part of the movement under control. Perform one set of 6 to 10 repetitions until failure.

Alternate Compound Exercises for the Chest

Bench Press

This exercise can be performed with a barbell, dumbbells, or a machine. I prefer using a machine as the guided mechanism provides greater control and there's no chance of getting stuck with a barbell on your chest in the event you fail in completing a rep. No matter which device you use, start with the weight at arms' length with your elbows locked (some machines require that you start with the weight in the bottom position). Your hands should be spaced slightly closer than shoulder width, with the elbows flared away from the torso, back toward the ears. Under very strict control, lower the weight to the upper part of the chest, just in front of the clavicles, or shoulder bones. With little pause, press back to the top where

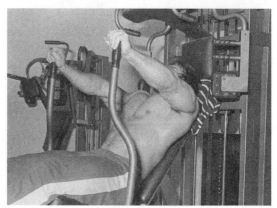

Machine chest presses are a good substitute for incline presses. Here Mentzer performs the Nautilus machine bench press as part of his pre-exhaust chest cycle.

the arms are straight and elbows locked; then lower under control. Perform one set of 1 to 3 repetitions until failure.

If using a barbell, I strongly suggest you have a spotter present in the event you fail completing a rep and/or have trouble racking the bar.

Dips

Take hold of the handles on a set of dipping bars and press yourself up to the top lock-out position so that your body weight is supported by your arms. Slowly lower yourself down until you feel a comfortable stretch in your pectoral muscles and then after a brief pause, press

Dips are also a great chest exercise when used as part of a pre-exhaust cycle.

yourself back to the starting position. You can place more emphasis on the pecs by allowing your upper arms to flare out away from the torso—the exact opposite advice when using dips to stimulate the triceps. Perform 1 to 3 repetitions until failure. Most modern gyms have dipping machines with a selectorized weight stack to one side—where you sit on a seat and press down in dip fashion. This is great for those who are not initially strong enough to dip with their own body weight.

If you don't have access to such a device and are not yet strong enough to perform even one full range dip with body weight, use the same negative-only method suggested for chins. Stand on a bench or chair in front of the dip bars. Position yourself into the top straight-arm, locked-elbow position; and lower slowly—ideally for 7 to 10 seconds. After a while, you'll find negative-only dips very easy, and you'll be ready for regular, full range dips. While most use this exercise for triceps, it's wonderful for stimulating the pectorals and the frontal deltoids as well.

Alternate Isolation Exercises for the Back

Dumbbell Pullovers

Lie on your back on a flat bench with your feet on the floor. Use one dumbbell, holding it in both hands in a straight-arm position over your head. Lower the dumbbell as far back as possible behind your head. Pause briefly and then return to the starting position. Perform one set of 6 to 10 repetitions.

Nautilus Machine Pullovers

Sit erect inside the pullover machine and fasten the seat belt. Push down on the foot pedal to move the elbow pads into position so that you can place your upper arms on the pads. Allow the upper arms to be stretched behind as far as comfortable. Then press the pads and move the elbows to a position just behind the torso. Pause in this fully-contracted position for a moment and then control the return of your upper arms to the fully-stretched starting position. Perform one set of 6 to 10 repetitions.

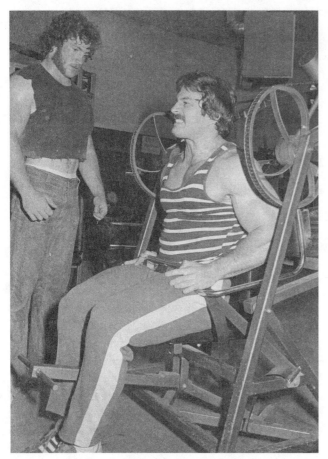

Nautilus machine pullovers provide direct resist-ance to the latissimus muscles of the upper back.

Barbell rows. Pull the bar straight up so that it hits your lower chest area.

Alternate Compound Exercises for the Back

Barbell Rows

This exercise can be done with a barbell, dumbbell, or a machine. Those with problem lower backs should use either a row machine or single-arm dumbbell rows. Most row machines have you sitting against a pad, taking all the stress off the lower back. Alternatively, using a dumbbell will allow you to support yourself with the free hand on the edge of a bench, reducing the stress on the lower back. For those using a barbell, stand directly behind the bar while bending over so your back is as flat as possible, parallel to the floor with your head up. Grasp the bar with a shoulder-width grip, and without changing your back position, rise up slightly so the barbell is not touching the floor. Then row, by pulling the bar straight up

so it hits the lower chest area. Because of the physics involved, this is one exercise in which you won't be able to hold the bar statically at the top of the movement. Just lower the bar under control, and repeat. Perform one set of 6 to 10 repetitions until failure.

One-Arm Dumbbell Rows

One-arm dumbbell rows are performed in essentially the same manner as the barbell row except you're supporting your torso with your free hand on the end of a bench or chair while rowing the dumbbell with your other hand. Row the dumbbell as high as you can—slightly above the plane of the torso—pause briefly, and lower under control. Perform one set of 6 to 10 repetitions until failure. Then rest as little as is required after completing the prescribed number of reps, and repeat with the other arm.

Chin-ups are a great upper body developer, particularly when employed as the compound portion of a pre-exhaust cycle.

One-arm dumbbell rows. Raise the dumbbell as high as you can—slightly above the plane of the torso—to ensure full contraction.

Rowing Machines

There are so many brands of rowing machines these days that it would be impossible to examine the proper use of each. However, the general principle with all of them is the same. While sitting upright on the seat pad, arch your back with your chest touching the pad directly in front of you. Grab the handles, and row under strict control. Once you're in as fully contracted a position as you can achieve, pause for two to three seconds and lower under control. Perform for one set of 6 to 10 repetitions until failure. This is primarily a latissimus exercise, but also hits the rear deltoids and the brachialis, the muscle on the outside of the arm between the biceps and triceps.

Chin-Ups

Take an underhand grip on an overhead chin-up bar. Allow your arms to hold your entire body weight. Next, draw your feet up behind your knees so that they are off the floor and slowly pull yourself up until your chin clears the top of the bar. Pause briefly in this fully-contracted position and then lower yourself

under control back to the starting position. Repeat for one set of 6 to 10 repetitions until failure.

If you are initially too weak to do a chin-up, start with negative-only chins. Next to the chin-up bar, place a bench or chair that is high enough so you can step right off of it into the top position where your chin is above the bar. Hold that position for a second or two, and lower very slowly, taking 5 to 10 seconds. If you can only do one lowering (or negative) rep at first, that's OK—negative reps improve strength rapidly, and you'll soon be doing regular, full-range reps. Upon reaching the bottom, stand back up on the bench or chair, reassume the top position of the chin, and perform another negative rep. Once you're able to do seven or more slow negatives, you should be able to start the full range reps where you lift (chin) yourself, pause, and lower under control. This exercise is employed to work primarily the latissimus, but is also effective in working the rear deltoids and in stimulating the biceps.

Alternate Exercise for Deadlifts

Shrugs

This exercise can be done with either a barbell, dumbbells, or a machine. I prefer the use of a machine as there is no need to pick the weights

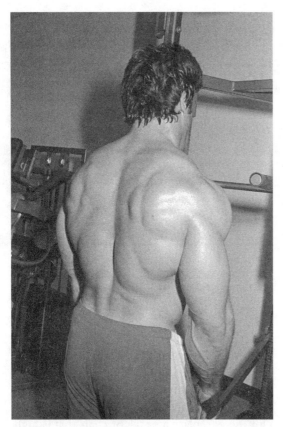 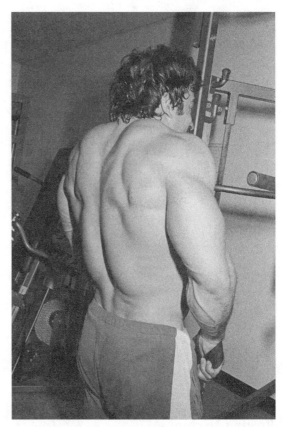

Shrugs can be performed with a barbell, dumbbells, a Universal bench press machine or, as pictured here, with a pair of straps and a floor pulley—the key is to raise your shoulders as high as possible.

off the floor; and the guided mechanism makes it less wieldy. Shrugs work primarily the trapezius, the muscles just off the shoulders, situated on the upper back. No matter which exercise device you use, start the movement with the weight at arms' length. Think of your arms as chains (straight up and down) with hooks on the ends (your hands). Without bending your arms, merely shrug your shoulders straight up toward your ears as far as they'll go—there's no rolling of the shoulders. If your back is rounded, the traps cannot be contracted fully. Hold the top position for a couple of seconds and then lower under control. Perform one set of 6 to 10 repetitions until failure. If you don't know how to use wrist straps, I'd advise you to learn soon. Once the weights you handle in this exercise start getting heavy, your grip will give out before you can reach a point of failure.

Note: As the deadlift exercise works not only the lower and upper back, but also the

hamstrings (commonly referred to as the leg biceps) on the back of the thighs, if you do not perform deadlifts you should make sure to include a set of leg curls with your leg training exercises during Workout One.

Leg Curls

The leg curl requires a special machine found in practically 100 percent of all commercial gyms. Lie face down on the machine in a position so that your Achilles tendons are braced under the pad of the movement arm and the knees are on the edge of the bench. Initiate the movement deliberately, with no sudden jerking or thrusting to get the weight started. Proceed likewise in a deliberate manner until you have curled your lower legs as high as they can go; until the movement arm pads touch the buttocks (if possible). Pause for two or three seconds in the top position; and lower under control. Repeat for 12 to 20 repetitions until

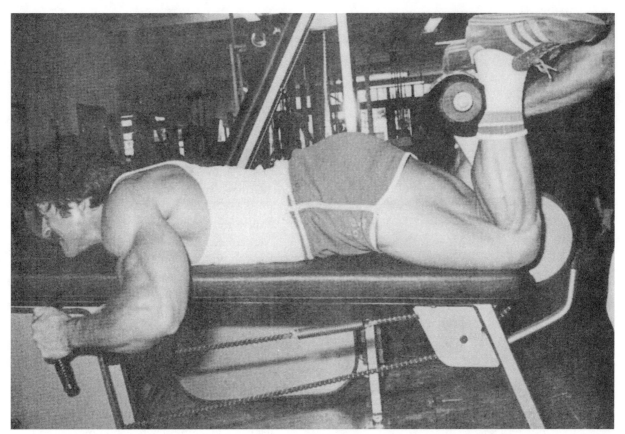

Leg curls—curl the legs as high as they can go and hold the fully contracted position for a distinct pause before lowering the resistance.

failure. Deadlifts also work well in stimulating the hamstrings, which is why the suggested workout has eliminated leg curls, thereby eliminating unnecessary, undesirable overlapping.

ALTERNATE EXERCISES FOR WORKOUT TWO: LEGS, CALVES, AND ABDOMINALS

Alternate Isolation Exercises for the Legs

The leg extension machine is the only exercise that effectively isolates the frontal thighs; therefore no substitutions are possible for this exercise.

Alternate Compound Exercise for the Legs

Squats

If you don't have a leg press machine, you can substitute the performance of a set of squats

In this kneeling abdominal pose, Mentzer's calves, hamstrings, quadriceps, and abdominals are shown to great effect—note the fanlike development of his serratus and intercostal muscles!

Squats—make sure you do not drop into or pause in the bottom position of the movement. If you need to rest briefly, do so at the top when your legs are fully extended.

fashion with your back flat and head up until the thighs are parallel to the ground, and no lower. Then immediately, without any bouncing, begin a controlled ascent to the top, straight-legged position. Once you've reached the top, pause only long enough to take a deep breath. Repeat. This works all of the thigh muscles together, though primarily the frontal quad muscles, and, as you'll discover, serves to greatly stimulate the cardiovascular system. *Warning*: Do not drop rapidly into a rock-bottom position where your buttocks are almost touching the ground and then bounce back up. Such a loose style of performance is a surefire prescription for injury. Remember: this is high-intensity, low-force exercise, the ideal, safest exercise possible when done correctly!

Alternate Compound Exercise for the Calves

Toe Presses

My favorite calf exercise is the toe press on the leg press machine. There is no pressure on the back with this one, and the weight seems more direct, as it passes right from the foot into the lower leg. Place the balls of the feet on the leg press and keep the knees locked while performing this exercise. The foot should be allowed to stretch back as far as possible before starting the toe press. From there the weight should move deliberately to a fully contracted position and be held for a pause before returning slowly to the bottom stretched position. Perform one set of 12 to 20 repetitions until failure.

Negative-accentuated exercise can be done here also. Be careful not to do more than one set of this exercise in negative-accentuated style the first time you try it. Negative resistance makes the muscles very sore, and the calves especially can become so sore from negatives that you won't be able to walk for a week if you aren't cautious.

immediately after the leg extension to complete the pre-exhaust cycle. As the squats involve the use of much heavier weights and can be dangerous to the lower back if proper caution isn't exercised, it is best to choose a weight that allows approximately 12 repetitions and stop at the point of positive failure rather than go on to total failure with forced and negative repetitions. Also, the use of a power rack with strong safety pins or a special machine with safety catches (such as a Smith Machine) is advised.

Place the bar on the upper back, below the nape of the neck, across the trapezius. With feet slightly wider than shoulder width and angled outward, descend in deep-knee-bend

Donkey Calf Raises

This is an old-time calf exercise that has endured owing to its effectiveness in building

Toe presses can be performed on any leg press machine—be sure to hold the fully contracted position briefly before lowering the resistance.

great calves. While not as practical an exercise to perform as the ones already indicated, owing to the fact that it requires another individual to sit on your lower back and (if your calves are quite strong) perhaps hold a heavy barbell plate on their lap, it is nevertheless a very potent exercise for stimulating the calves when performed properly.

Place your heels on a block of wood so that your calves can lower below a parallel position with the balls of your feet. Lean over and place your forearms onto a padded flat bench that should be elevated to a level so that your torso is bent forward at no more than a 90-degree angle to your legs. Have your assistant or training partner climb onto your lower back and sit up straight so that the resistance of his body weight is directly above your hips. Slowly, using only the strength of your calf muscles, rise up on tiptoes, making sure to flex your calves maximally at the top or fully-contracted position. Pause for a moment and then lower your heels back down into the pre-stretched starting position. Perform one set of 12 to 20 repetitions until failure.

Donkey calf raises—get a full contraction at the end of each repetition.

Alternate Exercises for the Abdominals

Hanging Leg Raises

Hanging by your hands from a chinning bar, raise your legs with knees straight until your feet touch the bar. Then lower your legs very strictly under control. It won't be necessary to use weight when you first utilize this exercise, but once you can perform one set of 20 repetitions, you will want to add some resistance to your feet to make the exercise more intense and progressive.

A good set of abdominals are crucial for competition as the abs are readily apparent even in transitions between poses.

ALTERNATE EXERCISES FOR WORKOUT THREE: SHOULDERS AND ARMS

Alternate Isolation Exercises for the Shoulders

Nautilus Lateral Raises

When I was training for the Mr. Olympia contest, this machine formed the core of my shoulder training. It actually is a machine that was engineered with the pre-exhaust principle firmly in mind as it has both a lateral (isolation) raise and press (compound) function incorporated into its mechanics. To begin the lateral raise portion, sit down in the machine with your back flat against the pad. Place your hands on the handles with the backs of your wrists flush against the pads on the movement arms. Slowly, by the strength of your shoulders

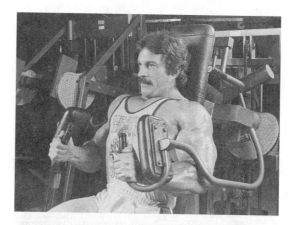

Nautilus lateral raises formed the core of Mike Mentzer's shoulder training when he was training for the Mr. Universe and Mr. Olympia contests.

alone, raise the movement arms up until they are parallel with your shoulders. Pause briefly in this fully contracted position and then lower the resistance slowly under control back to the starting position. Perform one set of 6 to 10 repetitions until failure.

Bent-Over Cable Laterals

Stand between two overhead pulleys and take hold of the handle for the pulley on your left with your right hand and the pulley on your right with your left hand. Bending over at the waist at a 90-degree angle and with your arms only slightly bent, draw your arms up and back until they are just behind your torso. Hold briefly in this fully contracted position and then lower slowly under control. Perform one set of 6 to 10 repetitions until failure.

Compound Exercises for the Shoulders

Upright Rows

This one involves the biceps, traps, and the anterior and lateral heads of the deltoid. Use a shoulder-width grip and raise the bar to nipple level, pause, and lower. Don't use so much weight that you start swinging it up. Bending back will give you a leverage advantage, so keep a straight back while performing this exercise. Straps will come in handy with this one, so you'd better get a pair. The forearms are involved in all exercises where you must grasp a bar with the hands, and they will become very pumped and fatigued when you perform those exercises to failure. After a few workouts on this system you'll understand why there is no need for direct forearm work. It's been said that I have the best forearms in the business, and I never did any direct forearm work!

Press Behind Neck

This most widely-practiced of all shoulder exercises is my personal favorite and has probably contributed more to my deltoid development than any other. It works all three delt heads (most particularly the anterior and lat-

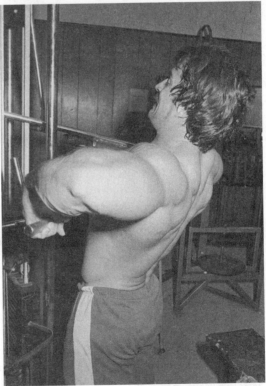

Upright rows can be performed to good effect with a barbell, straps, and a floor pulley or, as pictured, on a Universal machine. Lift your elbows up as high as possible.

Press behind neck—an exercise that hits all heads of the deltoids in addition to the trapezius, upper back, and triceps.

The press behind neck can also be performed on certain types of exercise machines, such as the Universal shoulder press machine Mike is using in this photograph.

Machine presses such as Nautilus are also excellent finishing movements after pre-exhausting the deltoids with a set of lateral raises.

eral heads) as well as the trapezius, upper back, and triceps.

There are numerous shoulder pressing machines, most noteworthy being the compound or pressing component of the Nautilus double shoulder machine. In using a barbell, take a shoulder-width grip in this exercise and keep the elbows directed to the sides so that the resistance is directed onto the delts as much as possible. Perform the movement in a slow and deliberate manner, pausing at the top before lowering under control. Repeat for one set of 6 to 10 repetitions until failure. Negatives can be done by jerking the weight to the top position. When doing the negatives, make sure that the weight is lowered slowly over the entire range of motion, and that you don't lose control of the weight once it has reached the maximum resistance point on its downward progression.

Machine Presses

Sit down with your back flat against the pad. Take hold of the handles and press upwards.

Make it a point to keep the elbows directed to the sides so that the resistance is directed onto the delts as much as possible. Perform the movement in a slow and deliberate manner, pausing at the top before lowering under control. Repeat for one set of 6 to 10 repetitions until failure.

Alternate Biceps Exercises

Standing Barbell Curls

Since most gyms have curling machines with mechanical physics that render them almost useless, I suggest the standard, straight-bar, barbell curl. The regular barbell curl is probably the simplest of the arm exercises to perform but also one of the most productive. It is easy to slip into a very loose style when doing the regular curl, so be especially cautious here to perform your first six reps with no sudden jerk or cheat.

Standing behind the bar, bend down with your back straight and head up. Grasp the bar with a shoulder-width grip and stand up. Without any sudden jerking, yanking, or thrusting to get the weight started, curl the bar under strict control while keeping your elbows tucked in at the waist. Allow the arms to extend fully at the bottom and curl all the way to the contracted position where the bar touches the clavicles. Upon reaching the top, pause only slightly and lower under control. On the last two or so hard reps it's all right to use a slight hitch to get the weight started, but

be sure to muscle it up as much as possible. Keep the elbows stable and tucked in to your sides with the hands held slightly wider. You will notice that the hardest part of the curl is at the point when the forearms are in a position perfectly parallel to the floor. This is the only point in the range of motion where you have direct resistance because here you will be pulling straight up, while the bar is being pulled straight down. It is important that you fight the weight through that point, rather than lean back with the body as leverage to help. Perform one set of 6 to 10 repetitions until failure. When the set is completed, replace the bar back on the floor carefully, with your back straight and head up.

Preacher Curls

This exercise has supplanted the regular barbell curl as the most popular arm exercise, due largely to its association with Larry Scott, the first winner of the Mr. Olympia contest (in 1965) and the man many believe to have had the most perfectly developed biceps of all time. It can be a very productive exercise for anyone if performed correctly.

Standing barbell curls are one of the most productive biceps exercises you can perform—if you perform them properly.

Preacher curls—for best results perform this exercise on a bench that has a slope of 90 degrees; this will ensure resistance in the position of full or peak contraction.

When doing this exercise, use a bench that has a slope of 90 degrees, or is perfectly perpendicular to the ground. This will ensure resistance at the top of the curl, which will greatly enhance the stimulation the biceps receive. The elbows should be pulled in as tight as possible, with the hands positioned slightly wider than the elbows, causing the forearms to form a V shape. Allow the arms to extend fully at the bottom of the movement, but be careful not to jerk the weight out of that position. Curl the weight slowly and deliberately from the bottom, pausing momentarily at the top before lowering slowly. Perform one set of 6 to 10 repetitions until failure.

Concentration curls—a great biceps builder that allows you to give yourself forced reps and negative reps with your free hand once a stage of positive muscular failure has been reached.

Palms-Up Chins

No, this exercise didn't get into the biceps section by accident. The biceps receive a lot of stimulation from this exercise, much like the close-grip pulldown.

Take an underhand grip on an overhead chin-up bar. Allow your arms to hold your entire body weight. Next, draw your feet up behind your knees so that they are off the floor and slowly pull yourself up until your chin clears the top of the bar. Pause briefly in this fully contracted position and then lower yourself under control back to the starting position. Repeat for one set of 6 to 10 repetitions until failure.

If you find it impossible to do chins, do them in a negative fashion. Using a box or chair, jump into the top position of the chin and lower yourself as slowly as possible all the way down to a completely stretched position. Do them until you can no longer control the downward motion of your body. After several workouts, you should have developed enough strength to perform at least a couple of regular positive chins. Continue with the negatives until you have sufficient strength to do six positive reps.

Concentration Curls

When I was training for the 1976 Mr. America contest, the Air Force base where I was stationed had but one exercise machine—a Marcy

Circuit Trainer—and a 45-pound dumbbell. I ended up using that dumbbell for concentration curls, which became the staple of my biceps training.

Begin the curl by taking hold of a dumbbell with your right hand with your arm hanging perpendicular and resting against the inside of your right thigh. From this "dead-hang" position, slowly curl the dumbbell up toward your left shoulder. As you proceed through the range of motion, supinate your hand so that the inside plate of the dumbbell touches the anterior delt of your left shoulder at the point of completion. Pause briefly in the fully contracted position and then lower the weight slowly under control. Perform one set of 6 to 10 repetitions until failure and then switch arms and repeat the procedure just described.

Nautilus Machine Curls

Sit down in the Nautilus curl machine and place your elbows on the pad in front of you. You should set the seat so that the pad is approximately level with your shoulders. Grasp hold of the handles and curl both arms up into the position of full contraction. Hold this position briefly before slowly lowering the weight back to the starting position. Perform one set of 6 to 10 repetitions until failure.

Note: This exercise can also be performed unilaterally (one arm at a time), which sometimes will serve to enhance your focus and concentration during the exercise.

Alternate Isolation Exercises for the Triceps

Lying Triceps Extensions

This is a great exercise for working the bulk of triceps at the top part of the arm.

With the head held off the edge of a bench for greater stretch in the extended position, and your arms locked out as if performing a bench press, let the bar down slowly from a position over the forehead slightly below the plane of the bench. Be careful to extend the forearms slowly with no sudden thrust back to the starting position. The elbows tend to be a delicate articulation and any sudden movements from the extended position can cause

Lying triceps extensions—be careful to extend the forearms slowly with no sudden thrust back to the starting position.

severe injury to the area, especially when appreciable weights are being handled. Pause briefly in this extended position and then press the weight back slowly to the starting position. Perform one set of 6 to 10 repetitions until failure.

Nautilus Triceps Extensions

Sit down in the Nautilus triceps machine so that your back is against the pad. Place your hands and elbows on the pads provided. Slowly extend both arms forward until full contraction. Pause in this position and then lower the handles back to the starting position. Perform one set of 6 to 10 repetitions until failure.

Note: This exercise can also be performed unilaterally (one arm at a time), which sometimes will serve to enhance your focus and concentration during the exercise.

French Presses

Taking hold of a barbell, press it overhead to arms' length. From this position, slowly lower the barbell to a point just behind your neck. Make sure that you keep your elbows stationary and as close to your ears as possible throughout the movement. Pause briefly in this fully stretched position and then press the bar back to the starting position. Perform one set of 6 to 10 repetitions until failure.

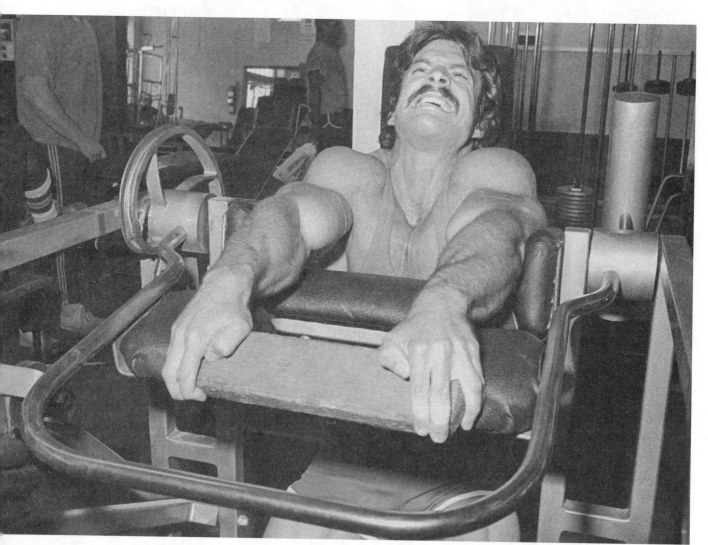

Nautilus triceps extensions—a great source of direct triceps stimulation.

French presses can be executed to good effect either while standing, sitting, or kneeling.

Alternate Compound Exercises for the Triceps

Close-Grip Bench Presses

Lying down on a flat bench, take hold of a barbell with a close grip (your hands should be approximately four inches apart) and lower it slowly to the midpoint of your chest. Pause briefly in this position and then press the weight back to arms' length. Perform one set of 3 to 5 repetitions until failure. This is a good alternative exercise for the triceps.

As you get bigger and stronger, the likelihood of overtraining looms greater, with the result that you must cut back further on the volume of your training.

Chapter 15

ADVANCED (CONSOLIDATED) TRAINING

In the years that I was a competitive body-builder seeking more intense ways to train in order to stimulate increases in muscle size, and in the years that followed in which I've been teaching others how to do the same, I've learned that plateaus, or sticking points, in progress are not inevitable. As you continue to grow stronger week to week, you find yourself lifting progressively heavier weights, which means that the stress you are placing on your recuperative subsystems is increasing as well. According to the principles of high-intensity training, unless you periodically insert another rest day or two to compensate for the ongoing, increasing stresses, the stresses will eventually reach a critical point and constitute overtraining. This in turn will cause a slowdown in progress and then a cessation of progress entirely. After a time, depending on the individual's rate of progress and the efficiency of his particular recovery ability, he would of necessity have to reduce his training to once every six to seven days as his regular regimen.

This last point, I have come to discover, is one of the most crucially important elements of anaerobic exercise science, and until now has been completely overlooked by everyone. Every other bodybuilding theorist—high-intensity or otherwise—has the trainee stay on the same volume and frequency protocol virtually forever. Once the fundamental principles are understood, the issue of progressively decreasing the volume and especially the frequency becomes the most pressing issue. If the bodybuilder bears this in mind, he will never reach a sticking point, there will be no need to engage in such protocols as periodization (wherein you train efficiently, i.e., intensely, for certain periods of time and then train inefficiently, i.e., with less intensity, for other periods), and he will actualize his muscular potential in a relatively short time.

The workouts prescribed in Chapter 13 will yield meaningful increases for the majority immediately. But for those who have advanced up the ladder of intensity into something approximating their genetic potential, this routine could well constitute overtraining, resulting in a cessation of the trainee's progress. Other people, those with poor innate recovery ability, may also find the recommended workout too taxing to produce much in the way of worthwhile results. If after two and no more than three complete cycles of the four-workout protocol little or no strength increase is witnessed, cease the routine entirely.

If a given routine is ever going to be productive, it should begin to yield meaningful results immediately. If you are not seeing results immediately with this routine or if you have come to a momentary halt in your progress after two to three complete cycles of the four-workout protocol, take a two week layoff and resume training with the workout program in this chapter.

Of course, those with average to superior recovery ability undoubtedly witness strength increases right from the beginning while using the prescribed workout routine. And if they follow the advice, their progress should be uninterrupted for months. I can't say precisely how long because the genetics of recovery ability varies across a broad (and highly individual) continuum.

CONSOLIDATION WORKOUTS

However good the progress, if the individual has regulated the frequency downward to the point where he is now working out only once every six to seven days, and no strength increases are witnessed for two or three cycles, he should cease that routine entirely. A complete cessation of progress means that the increases continued over a period of time so that the associated stress/demands—given the volume and frequency protocol—reached a critical point where they constituted overtraining. A sticking point may be prevented by taking a two-week layoff when a slowdown in progress is experienced. And after the layoff, resume training on a routine that excludes some of the specialized isolation movements (i.e., omit the dumbbell flyes, straight-arm pulldowns, leg extensions, and triceps extensions) and focuses on compound movements (dips, squats, pulldowns, etc.) that activate more muscle mass. The following is just such a program. (Because I have indicated the proper exercise protocol for each of the following exercises in Chapters 13 and 14, I will simply present the consolidation workouts in schematic form.)

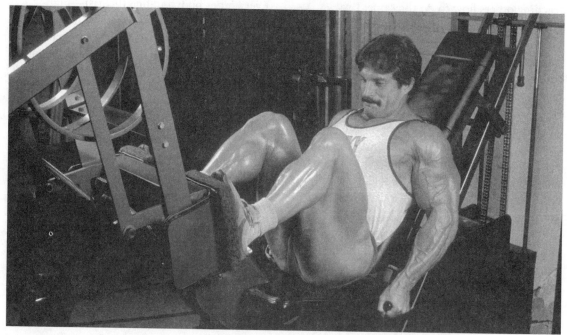

Leg presses can be alternated for squats periodically in the consolidation routine.

Close-grip, palms-up chins will work not only the biceps, but also the lats, shoulders, abs, and pecs.

Press behind neck will hit almost all of the upper body muscles, which together with the deadlift makes for a complete body workout without fear of overlapping.

Workout One

Squats (alternated periodically with leg presses)	1 × 12–20 reps
Close-grip, palms-up pulldowns	1 × 6–10 reps
Dips	1 × 6–10 reps

Workout Two

Deadlifts (alternated periodically with shrugs)	1 × 6–10 reps
Press behind neck	1 × 6–10 reps
Standing calf raises	1 × 12–20 reps

These two workouts should be conducted with five or six days of rest separating them. And as you grow stronger over time, begin inserting an extra rest day or two at random. Continue to insert the added rest day(s) with greater regularity until you are training but once every six to seven days—or less—if and

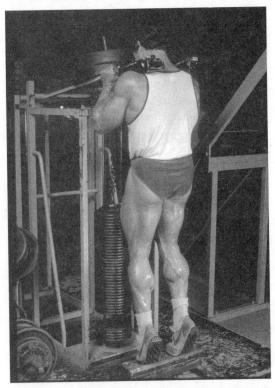

Standing calf raises will ensure that your lower legs are adequately stimulated in the consolidation routine.

when you deem such to be necessary for full recovery and overcompensation to take place.

The exercises may be changed periodically. For instance, leg presses may be substituted for squats; incline presses may be used in the place of dips; and Nautilus presses will serve well in place of the press behind neck. The important thing to bear in mind is that this is a consolidation program wherein isolation exercises that work single muscles, or parts of muscles, are eliminated. The focus here is on compound exercises that activate as much muscle mass as possible.

This advanced workout program is designed to eliminate as much overlapping as possible while still stimulating maximum growth in all of the major skeletal muscles. Also, this routine stimulates maximum growth with the absolute minimum amount of exercise possible, thereby making the least inroad into recovery ability possible, and thus making more of the body's limited reserve of resources available for growth production. Curls for the biceps are not included because, as mentioned earlier, the close-grip, palms-up pulldowns will more than suffice to stimulate growth in the lats and biceps. And the dips will be perfectly adequate to stimulate growth in the pecs as well as the deltoids and triceps. The deadlift is the greatest overall growth exercise as it works every muscle on the backside of the body, from the Achilles tendon to the occiput of the head. Deadlifts also work the deltoids, the forearms, and just about every muscle in the body.

With a consolidation routine such as this, especially for the more advanced bodybuilder, I advocate the more regular use of advanced techniques such as forced reps, cheat reps, negatives, partials, static contraction, and rest-pause. The individual will have to determine their use. For weight selection, number of reps, rest between sets, etc., please refer to the first list of high-intensity training principles in Chapter 11.

THE DYNAMICS OF PHYSICAL CHANGE

During periods of progress (i.e., increasing strength and muscle mass), one's physiology is not static, but in a continual process of change. And as the individual's body progresses, or changes, his training requirements change. Once the fundamentals of intensity, volume, and frequency are understood, this issue of changing training requirements follows as the most crucially important issue in exercise science.

If you desire unbreached progress, you must keep in mind all the while that as you continue to grow stronger and lift progressively heavier weights, the stresses grow greater—and they must be compensated for. If you could perform 5 reps to failure on the pulldowns in one workout and, in the very next workout on that same exercise, you performed 10 reps to failure, something doubled. When performing twice as many reps with the same weight it can be said that the individual doubled, or increased by 100 percent, his work output; having done so, he also increased the stress. He did not necessarily double the stress, however, because as his work capacity and strength increase, so do his anaerobic fitness and endurance, which enables the individual to tolerate more demanding workouts better, i.e., less stressfully. In a scientific, physiologic sense, less stressfully means with less actual wear and tear on the body. This is not to say that the stresses don't increase at all. They most certainly do, as evidenced by a trainee's progress slowing down when he doesn't sufficiently compensate for the increasing stresses by adequately reducing volume and frequency in a timely fashion.

Slowdowns or halts in progress are typically the result of a particular volume and frequency protocol eventually amounting to undertraining. Proof of this is the fact that concomitant with the slowdown or halt in progress are the onset of other symptoms of overtraining. Most remarkable of these is the fact that the individual, prior to the slowdown, felt fully recovered, teeming with energy, and possessed an abundance of motivation going into the gym for his workouts. Now, given the same volume and frequency protocol, he doesn't feel adequately recovered between workouts and experiences a lingering fatigue and a reduction in motivation. The key to uninterrupted progress, therefore, is to remain

"During periods of increasing strength and muscle mass, one's physiology is not static, but in a continual process of change."—Mike Mentzer

As you continue to get bigger and stronger, you will have to make a concerted effort to cut back on the length of your training sessions and to diminish the frequency of your training. This is the only way to allow the growth you stimulate to be produced.

aware of the above—and compensate for the ongoing, increasing stresses.

This consolidation program will put the advanced trainee—as well as the beginner with poor recovery ability—back onto a satisfying path of regular progress. For the advanced trainee with advanced development who has regulated the volume and frequency of his training down to three or four sets every six or seven days, this routine is his last stop on the road to the full actualization of his muscular potential.

The consolidation routine is the last stop on the road to realizing the full development of your muscular potential.

Mike Mentzer up against some of the greatest bodybuilders of all time (In the back row from left to right: Danny Padilla, Boyer Coe, Roy Duval, Roger Walker, and Roy Callender. In the front row from left to right: Arnold Schwarzenegger, Mentzer, Frank Zane, Dennis Tinerino.) at the 1980 Mr. Olympia contest.

Part V

CONCERNS FOR THE COMPETITIVE BODYBUILDER

Mike Mentzer, ripped to the bone in an absolute peak of condition at the 1980 Mr. Olympia contest.

Chapter 16

THE ART OF PEAKING
ENHANCING MUSCULAR DEFINITION

It's very difficult to peak at a predetermined date, and it requires specialized knowledge to do so. If you don't believe me, take a look at how many—or how few!—professional bodybuilders are able to consistently reach peak shape for our sport's greatest competitions.

As a bodybuilder, your first objective was to develop as much muscle mass as possible, distributing it uniformly over your entire body. But when you choose to reach peak muscularity on a set date, the acquisition of muscle mass ceases to be your primary concern. As you no doubt already know, the criteria used in judging physiques include absence of visible bodyfat, degree of muscle mass, proportional balance, symmetry, posing, and general appearance.

The first thing an inexperienced competitor must learn is to assess his existing condition so that he will have sufficient time to make the changes in training and diet necessary to peak. The length of time you will require to prepare for a competition will hinge largely on your existing bodyfat levels. The leaner you are

when you begin preparing for a contest, the less time you'll need. There are several ways in which you can learn how much of your body is fat, but the best and most accurate ones are rather expensive. The two most practical methods for bodybuilders are hydrostatic (underwater) weighing and skin-pinch caliper measurement.

HYDROSTATIC WEIGHING

Hydrostatic weighing involves being weighed both in the normal manner and underwater. Because muscle is more dense than water, a bodybuilder's lean body mass, or muscle, will sink and be weighed, while fat, which is less dense than water, will float and not be counted. Using standardized mathematical calculations, the difference between your normal weight and underwater weight will tell you how much of your body is made up of fat and how much is lean muscle tissue. Hydrostatic weighing tanks can usually be found on college campuses (in exercise physiology labs) and increasingly often at commercial establishments that perform physiological tests.

THE SKIN-PINCH CALIPER

The skin-pinch caliper method is much simpler but not always as accurate. The procedure involves measuring the thickness of skin folds at various points of the body, usually the biceps, triceps, and lower back. By comparing these values to a standardized chart, bodyfat levels can be determined. Calipers can be found in some pharmacies and all medical supply stores.

PERSONAL EXPERIENCE

Prior to competing in my second Mr. Olympia competition, I used hydrostatic weighing on a regular basis, and my calculations of caloric deficits created by dieting and aerobic activity brought me to my peak on time with no guesswork. By knowing how many pounds of fat you need to lose, you can calculate how long it will take to reach a ripped (highly defined) condition, which I define as a bodyfat composition of between three and six percent.

Of course, the simplest and least expensive method of assessing physical condition is to

"The simplest and least expensive method of assessing physical condition is to merely look in the mirror."—Mike Mentzer

merely look in the mirror. Are your chest muscles clearly delineated around the edges, giving your pecs a squared-off look? Can you grab fat in the nipple area, or is the skin tight and close to the muscle? What about the area around your navel? Does it jiggle or is it tight with no visible roll of fat? One area that provides an excellent indication of your overall condition is the lower back, right above the hips on either side of your spine. If you can grab an inch or more of fat in that area, you will probably need up to 10 weeks of rigid dieting to get ripped.

Before a competition, I frequently pinch the skin around my navel to see if it is thinning out. If it is and my muscle size and strength levels are intact, I continue what I've been doing. If not, I make the necessary adjustments in diet and aerobic activity. Five or six weeks should be the minimum length of time allocated for contest prep, while anything more than 10 to 12 weeks becomes too taxing on both mind and body. Look at fat loss logically: even on the most severe diet the maximum amount of fat you can possibly lose in one week is three pounds. At that rate, you would lose 18 pounds in six weeks, allowing no time for error or backsliding. Losing two pounds of fat a week is a more realistic goal, and it reduces the probability of losing muscle mass. If you try to lose fat too fast, you'll inevitably burn some muscle for energy.

PHYSICAL ACTIVITY AND BODYFAT LOSS

Let's consider physical activity and bodyfat loss. Though it's true that increased levels of physical activity burn more calories and leads to faster weight loss, weight training is not the best way to burn off fat. Your weight workouts should be used solely to maintain or increase muscle mass. Oxygen must be present in order for fat to be metabolized for energy. The demands for energy imposed by anaerobic activity—such as weight training or sprinting—are so great and immediate that oxygen can't be supplied rapidly enough to metabolize fat for that energy. It's only the sugar (called

Jogging one mile will burn more than 100 calories or roughly 15 calories per minute.

glycogen) stored within a muscle itself that can be metabolized in the absence of oxygen.

The best formula when preparing for a contest includes weight workouts that progressively decline in intensity the last two weeks prior to a show and aerobic activity that increases in duration and frequency over the final four to six weeks. At the start of your contest preparation period your weight training sessions should be very intense. As a result, your aerobic activity should be of relatively short duration, such as bicycle riding 6 to 10 miles at a slow to moderate pace once or twice a week, combined or alternated with jogging 1½ to two miles.

As the contest approaches, ridding your body of fat becomes the ever-increasing concern. Then the intensity of your training should decrease somewhat, while the duration of the aerobic, or fat-burning, activity increases. I would suggest cycling at least twice a week for 30 to 45 minutes and running up to three or more miles on two additional times during the week, on alternate days from when you perform your aerobic cycling sessions. I prefer running to cycling because it burns calories more quickly, but you may prefer cycling, as it is less traumatic to the knee and ankle joints. Jogging a mile burns 100 to 120 calories, or roughly 15 calories per minute, while cycling at a moderate pace (approximately 8 to 13 miles per hour) burns about 8 calories per minute.

Your aerobic training should be performed at what I call a relaxed pace; if you're gasping for breath while performing your aerobic exercise, that means you're increasing the proportion of sugar being burned for fuel and decreasing the use of bodyfat. If you can't talk easily while jogging or cycling, you're working too intensely. Perform your aerobics at a conversational pace, and you will be using up to 90 percent stored fat as fuel.

Diet is just as important as increased activity levels in getting you ripped. No matter how active you are, continuing to consume more calories than you burn will keep you from losing fat. The safest and most effective approach to dieting for a contest is to maintain a diet that's lower in calories. A well-balanced diet is composed of 60 percent carbohydrates, 25 percent proteins, and 15 percent fats, with the foods derived from the four basic food groups—meats, fruits and vegetables, dairy products, and grains and cereals.

Remember, as long as you take in fewer calories than you need to meet metabolic and physical activity energy requirements, you'll lose fat. If you require 3,000 calories a day to maintain your weight and all of a sudden you reduce this to 2,000 calories, you'll lose fat. The three macronutrients—protein, carbohydrates, and fats—all contain calories, and it is the eating of too many calories that results in the creation of fat on your body—and too many calories derived from protein sources will make you just as fat as too many calories from carbohydrates or fats. A calorie is a calorie, no matter what the source.

"As long as you take in fewer calories than you need to meet metabolic and physical activity energy requirements, you'll lose fat."—Mike Mentzer

To lose fat, simply reduce your calories to a lower daily figure. Don't be too drastic at the start. Begin by cutting 500 calories per day. As each week passes, reduce your food consumption by perhaps 200 more calories per day. This gradual reduction, coupled with progressively increased aerobic activity, will inevitably result in reaching peak shape on contest day—if you've properly assessed your initial physical condition and allowed yourself enough time to get cut up. Just consume a well-balanced, reduced-calorie diet, and you'll get ripped. An occasional ice-cream cone or piece of cake won't hurt, as long as you maintain a daily caloric intake below your personal maintenance levels.

You should continue to train as usual, in high-intensity style—no more than four workouts within every 20 days, one to two total sets per bodypart, and using high-intensity principles such as pre-exhaust, forced, and negative reps. But as I mentioned earlier, your energy levels, and hence your weight-training intensity, will have to decrease somewhat as contest time approaches. Three weeks out you can drop the negative reps from your routine and only occasionally do forced reps. Going only to positive failure on each set will maintain muscle mass, and for the last three weeks that will be enough because your only concern at that point is to maintain size while losing all visible bodyfat.

It is still important to train with high-intensity when dieting in order to maintain your muscle mass while you lose bodyfat. However, as gaining mass is no longer your priority, some of the high-intensity techniques should be discontinued the closer the contest becomes.

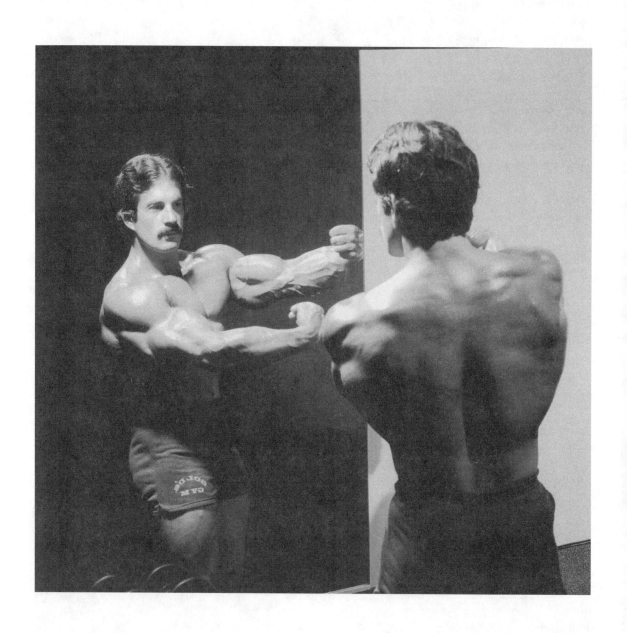

Chapter 17

YOUR MIRROR AND HOW TO USE IT

Because bodybuilders have long been characterized as narcissists mesmerized by their own reflections, the American public has always regarded them rather gingerly. And while it is undoubtedly true that some bodybuilders spend an inordinate amount of time ogling themselves in the mirror, the same can be said of many people.

Ironically, many serious bodybuilders are mirror-shy, actually reluctant to spend as much time in front of the glass as they should. The reason stems from their fear of being labeled narcissists and an ignorance of the necessity of using the mirror in their preparations.

THE NEED FOR AN OBJECTIVE MEASURE

In the movie *Pumping Iron*, Arnold Schwarzenegger made the astute observation that for the bodybuilder the mirror was analogous to the runner's stopwatch. Indeed, as competitive bodybuilding is a purely visual/aesthetic form, the individual athlete must possess some way of objectively assessing the level of his development, the degree of his definition, the parity of his proportions, the polish of his overall appearance and his ability to present his physique. This information must be readily available so he can make fine-tuning adjustments in his training and diet leading up to a contest. Still photos and videotape can be helpful, but as the impending competition grows closer and closer, only the mirror can provide him with the instantaneous feedback he requires.

The tape measure, the calipers, and the scales do not serve the same function as the mirror because the attributes they measure—girth, subcutaneous fat, and body weight—are not central to the competitive judging process, in which decisions are based on a composite analysis of physiques. While the aforementioned measuring devices can certainly be useful to the bodybuilder by providing specific, isolated bits of information about his present condition and his progress, only the mirror provides the overall picture integrating all of his physical attributes. Only the mirror gives him an instantaneous perceptual assessment of himself as others see him.

EFFECTIVE USE OF THE MIRROR

Although the mirror can be an enormously valuable tool, it can also be a trap you fall into, much like the pool that claimed Narcissus. The following points will help you avoid pitfalls while providing you with fuel to help skyrocket you to the outer limits of your bodybuilding potential:

• *Overcoming mirror-shyness.* For various reasons many bodybuilders find it difficult to

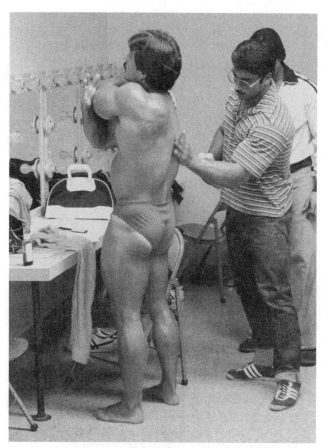

Bodybuilders use the mirror right up to the day of the competition. Here Mike Mentzer applies oil to his muscles while his brother Ray evens it out on Mike's upper back.

face a mirror while checking out their physiques or practicing their posing. These reasons include fear of being seen and labeled a narcissist, spotting flaws and imperfections, and the enormous effort required to use a mirror properly. Privacy and the proper attitude—discussed below—will help you overcome any such reluctance once you've recognized that you are, in fact, mirror-shy.

• *Avoiding mirror-dependency.* It is not uncommon for bodybuilders to be unable to practice individual poses and posing routines without the mirror. They're so dependent on their reflected image that they insist anyone who watches them do so only in the mirror. This implies they are not confident of their own perceptions or of their development and are afraid the other person might see something they can't see in the exact same position under the exact same lighting they're accustomed to. This, of course, is ridiculous. Be certain to practice individual poses and your entire routine without a mirror, beginning at least two weeks before competition.

• *Attitude—avoid the looking-glass blues.* No, your physique is not perfect yet. Everyone, including the top champs, can improve on some aspect of his physique, be it in size, definition, or symmetry. Don't become disgruntled, dispirited, or discombobulated because your definition isn't quite as good as so-and-so's. The mirror is there so you can accurately compare yourself to yourself, from time to time. If you really were expecting perfection, why look at all? Once you realize how much physical energy and mental focus are actually required to study yourself in each pose and to assess your current condition, there is often a reluctance to engage in future sessions before the mirror. Quite often future sessions are approached with the attitude "I've got to," depriving one of motivational fuel, and will end up a waste of time. However, if you focus on the value of such posing sessions, your attitude will quickly become one of "Let me at it!"

• *The importance of privacy.* When Gold's Gym added 4,000 square feet to their already spacious workout area recently, Pete Grymkow-

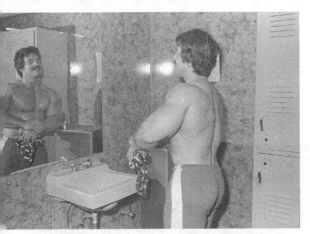

"The mirror is there so you can accurately compare yourself to yourself from time to time."—Mike Mentzer

ski, one of the owners, had the foresight and experience to include an 8 × 10-foot private posing room with track lights and full-length frontal mirror with another mirror set at an angle for viewing the back. A private area to practice your posing in front of a mirror is essential for concentration. If your gym doesn't have such an area, it is imperative that you arrange one in your own home, someplace where you can set up a full-length mirror, along with one for viewing your back. Without such privacy you'll fear others are watching and making comments, something you don't need, especially before a contest.

• *Essential details—mirrors, lights, and space.* In order to practice and perfect individual poses, a full-length mirror is mandatory. Striking a pose involves the entire physique, head to toe. If space and money allow, a specially angled mirror set up to view your back

poses would be helpful. And, of course, there must be enough space to move all your limbs—especially your arms—as you swing, stride, twist, and bend going from one pose to the next. If space is lacking, you'll feel inhibited and you'll be forced to cut short your movements during practice—and if you practice wrong, you'll perform likewise in competition. An overhead spotlight angled to light the legs along with the upper body is the least you should have in terms of lighting. Whatever you do, don't use a light that tends to cause you to look less than your best. Too harsh a light can cause a little bodyfat to appear magnified, while a dull, diffuse light will cause you to seem smaller and less muscular.

Shed your shyness and keep your ego in check, and your mirror can be as useful a tool in your contest preparations as any piece of exercise equipment.

Mike Mentzer hits a front lat spread pose, displaying the muscles of his upper back, chest, and shoulders.

Chapter 18

THE ART OF POSING

In addition to individual personality and temperament, each of us also possesses a unique assemblage of physical attributes. To be effective, a posing routine must complement those physical attributes and at the same time express the essence of the personality.

If you hope to do as well as possible in your physique competitions, without question you'll have to do your homework in the gym and pay strict attention to diet, but unless adequate time and energy are devoted to posing and presentation practice, you won't do as well as you might have in the final judging. It's not uncommon, in fact, to see a lesser physique triumph over a superior one because of a more polished stage presentation.

POSING—AN EXPRESSION OF WHO YOU ARE

The point is that the style of posing you adopt should serve as a complete expression of who *you* are, and the selection of appropriate poses is the first step in this process. In selecting your

Mentzer hits a side chest pose.

The "vacuum" pose.

poses, you must start out by assessing your physical stature. A person with a short, stocky physique similar to that of a diminutive Hercules would be foolhardy to attempt the ethereal moves more suitable to a lithe type of physique.

It's up to the individual to select his or her poses from the innumerable variety available to the imagination. A full repertoire should include shots from all basic views: front, back, and left and right sides. If you neglect to present your body from any of these views, the judges will automatically assume that you are hiding a weak point. After you have chosen the basics, add the more exotic kneeling, twisting, and striding poses. Limit yourself however to no more than 15 total poses. Any more than that will be boring and probably redundant in your routine. Next, incorporate all of these poses into a routine that allows for fluid and graceful transitions from one pose to the next.

Posing and presenting your physique properly requires considerable skill and represents the sport side of bodybuilding. However, posing also requires that you express your own individuality, which involves a certain amount of creativity and reflects the artistry of bodybuilding. As a so-called sport and/or art style, posing in bodybuilding demands the mastery of technical skills along with artistic renditions. To the degree that posing expresses how an individual feels about himself and his relationship to the audience, posing is a form of nonverbal communication. Hence, it's necessary to make each pose technically perfect, and this involves the proper placement of the hands, feet, and head. You also need the ability to simultaneously flex all the muscles involved and to display the appropriate facial expression.

ASPECTS OF EFFECTIVE POSING

As an art form, posing is still evolving, which means that there's infinite room for creativity. It is obvious from watching the more accomplished bodybuilding champions, however, that effective posing should appear effortless, relaxed, graceful, and enjoyable for the poser. Additionally, the transitions between each pose

must be free-flowing, with all bodyparts moving uniformly in a coordinated fashion. Most important, these transitions must reflect elements of the personality. However, infusing a posing routine with personality will require a great deal of practice and experience. It can't be taught. Nevertheless, I've formulated a list of 11 points that should help you to master the technical and artistic details of posing.

"When practicing, it is important to relax and focus your thoughts on the task at hand."—Mike Mentzer

"Experiment and alter your posing routines from contest to contest. As your physique and competitive nature evolve, so should your posing routine."
—Mike Mentzer

1. When practicing, it is important to relax and focus your thoughts on the task at hand. Select an environment that is quiet and free of outside distractions.

2. Set aside at least three half-hour periods a week for posing practice. As a contest nears, increase the frequency of your posing practice sessions. During the last week before the contest, you should decrease the frequency of your workouts or eliminate them altogether, as Arnold did, and substitute daily or even twice daily posing sessions. (Muscle contractions during posing are intense enough to substitute for workouts during this last week.) Don't perform any intense activity the last couple of days before a show. Relax, recuperate, and conserve your energy. Your routine must come as if it were second nature to you, so practice, practice, practice! Nothing looks worse than a bodybuilder who hesitates during her routine, which indicates that she's forgotten the sequence of her poses.

3. Get comfortable with the mirror. Although the previous chapter dealt exclusively with the significance of the mirror as an aid to your physique presentation and assessment, it bears repeating that few bodybuilders spend enough quality time in front of the mirror. Practicing the technical aspects of posing and analyzing the details of his appearance are extremely important to the competitive bodybuilder. The mirror-shy athlete must learn to relax in front of the mirror. It's the only way to improve posing and presentation.

4. Practicing in front of a mirror is essential, but don't limit your practice to the mirror. You don't want to become mirror-dependent—unable to pose without a mirror. On a regular basis, have a friend who is familiar with posing and physique competition watch your routine and offer critical comments. This will help you to correct any mistakes you may have overlooked while practicing alone.

5. If possible, have a competent photographer shoot stills of your routine. This will enable you to analyze each pose for technical details, making sure hands, feet, and head are all properly positioned. (Photos taken during competition will also provide material for future analysis and further upgrading of your appearance and routine.) Also, now that video is generally available, I strongly suggest you use it—in addition to still photos—to check yourself. The advantage of video is that it can provide instantaneous feedback of your practice, enabling you to correct mistakes before they become habits.

6. Experiment and alter your posing routines from contest to contest. As your physique and competitive nature evolve, so should your posing routine. Years of practice, experience, and experimentation are necessary before you

Mike Mentzer bids his fans adieu at the conclusion of his posing routine at the 1980 Mr. Olympia contest in Australia. He would never compete in the Mr. Olympia again.

"In addition to displaying your physical assets, it's important to exhibit a confident stage presence."
—Mike Mentzer

can hope to express yourself maturely and fully through posing.

7. Since posing is a form of nonverbal communication, you must learn to talk to the audience with your body. Your onstage body language will affect the judges and the audience on both the conscious and the unconscious levels. The fact is, the very moment you appear onstage you begin conveying impressions to everyone. By being keenly aware of this phenomenon, you can purposely control what you communicate. In addition to displaying your physical assets, it's important to exhibit a confident stage presence. Any expression of nervousness, uncertainty, or self-consciousness will cause you to appear weak and will affect the judges' decision. The audience, too, is very

sensitive and will pick up on any negative emotions. If you are in your best possible condition and have done your posing homework, you should appear proud, confident, and happy. These feelings will be expressed naturally in your posing, all of which can be effectively topped off with a heartfelt smile as you make your exit.

8. Equally important as your posing and presentation is your overall appearance. Judging a physique is akin to judging a thoroughbred horse. Nothing escapes scrutiny. Things such as skin texture, grooming, attire, and posture paint a composite picture. Give yourself at least four to six weeks to work on a suntan. This will be enough time to develop a rich, even color rather than the blotchy, red job that a rush tan or a sun lamp can create.

9. Take good care of your skin as well. After your workouts, take a warm shower and use a mild soap. If you have problems with blemishes, see a dermatologist. Also, get a haircut to suit your head and physique. Too much hair will enlarge the head and detract from your shoulder width. A trim haircut is best.

10. In addition to the hair being well groomed, the condition of the face is extremely important. Mustaches may enhance certain facial types, but beards almost always detract. Be discriminating in either case. Take good care of your teeth, brushing after each meal and avoiding refined sugars in your diet. If your teeth are less than pearly white, have them professionally cleaned.

11. Either buy an appropriately cut pair of posing trunks or have them custom made. If you have a long torso, your trunks should ride relatively high on your waist. If you are short, then your trunks should be cut lower so that your physique presents a more elongated appearance. If your thighs are short, then your trunks should be cut high on the thighs; for those with longer legs, trunks should be cut lower. If you enter the contest with a deep, bronze skin tone, then the color of your trunks can range from pale yellow to a hotter color like red. Lighter skin tones, on the other hand, require suits that are in earth tones like brown and green.

"If you are in your best possible condition and have done your posing homework, you should appear proud, confident, and happy."—Mike Mentzer

TIME AND PRACTICE

As I've already written, developing a competent, mature posing routine and stage presence requires time and lots of practice. There's a lot of information in this chapter and implementing all of it will take time and practice. I can't reiterate their significance enough. Don't skimp on either one, and the rewards that you gain will be commensurate.

Part VI

MOTIVATION AND PSYCHOLOGY

A siege mentality is required if a bodybuilder hopes to realize the most from his workouts and become a champion.

Chapter 19

DEVELOPING A SIEGE MENTALITY IN THE GYM

How many of you have been following an impeccable diet, training with the latest high-intensity principles such as pre-exhaustion and static contraction, and are still not progressing at a satisfactory rate?

In such cases I strongly suspect that the culprit is the attitude the bodybuilder carries with him to the gym. Many come into the gym in the evening, for instance, feeling defeated, perhaps having been royally chewed out by their bosses just an hour earlier. Their workouts will most likely end up wishy-washy affairs, lacking the ferocious intensity required for optimal progress. What is required if a bodybuilder hopes to realize the most from his workouts and become a champion? The answer: an attitude befitting a hero, one full of fury—an attitude I call *siege mentality*. Once he enters the gym, all else is forgotten and he is transformed into a valiant warrior with girded loins, ready to do battle with the weights.

Although we are loath to admit it, the human race is by nature bellicose. History books are chronicles of our conflicts since Day One. And as much as our society decries the horrors of war, few would have our nation's past military glory erased from the history books. In ancient times, of course, men were hunters, and the most profitable and exciting way to live was to attack a neighboring tribe, kill its men, take its women, and loot its villages. Because the more aggressive people endured, humankind's bellicose instincts have survived. The human race has evolved through struggle and combat. A life devoid of effort or struggle is enervating. Indeed, so much of civilized life today, while bestowing a certain amount of security, at the same time has withheld adventure.

Lacking a sufficient outlet for our biological drives and aggressive instincts, we are afflicted with depression and other nervous suffering—and no wonder! To flourish, the will needs a rallying point. At one time warfare gave individuals and societies that rallying point. But modern war is untenable. For myself and countless others, athletic training and sports competition provide a functional alternative to warfare.

Sport psychologists and social commentators have long noted the value of sports as an outlet for humankind's more aggressive—even murderous—drives. Nat Hentoff wrote in the *Atlantic Monthly* that tennis provided an outlet for his frustrated need to express power and his murderous instincts. "Better health through murder, and the corpses can easily be replaced in tins of three," wrote Hentoff. In fact, the original purpose of sports was to toughen the individual physically and psychologically for warfare.

RELEASE FROM ANXIETY

When I was a competitor I found that during the off-season, when I was relatively inactive, my anxiety level increased and life in general seemed more problematic. As soon as I was faced with the impending challenge of a major physique competition however, my entire psyche underwent a profound change. My anxiety level dropped to zero and the sense of laziness and vague discontent evaporated. Everything around me—people, things, ideas—assumed a heightened sense of meaning and purpose. Like the French philosopher Jean-Paul Sartre, who said he never felt more alive than when he was fighting the Germans in World War II, I've always found life easiest when it's hardest; that

"I've always found life easiest when it's hardest; that is, when the greatest demands and privations are required."—Mike Mentzer

is, when the greatest demands and privations are required.

The psychologist William James noted: "It is sweat and effort, human nature strained to its utmost and on the rack, yet getting through alive, which inspire us." I always considered preparing for a contest to be my moral equivalent to war. Once contest preparation commenced, the gym ceased to be a mundane menagerie of grunting humans and was transformed into a mythical battlefield where the militaristic virtues of sweat, discipline, and physical courage were applauded. The gym became an arena where I had the opportunity to be a hero.

The night before each workout, my brother Ray and I would meet to plan our strategy for the next day's assault on immortality. Like supreme military commanders planning a massive attack, we would pore over our training journals, deciding which exercises and training principles were needed for a particular body part and which scheme of sets and reps would work the best. During this nighttime summit and the next morning before the training session, Ray and I would go about deliberately cultivating an aggressive warlike attitude that would carry over into the workout.

Reading also serves the purpose of helping to foster a more aggressive attitude in the gym. When I won the Mr. Universe contest in Acapulco in 1978, my "training partner" during my workouts was—and this is meant somewhat facetiously—Friedrich Nietzsche. I was reading his works four to five hours a day before the contest. Reading him put me in a certain state of mind and being. He intensified my state of being as he was a very intense writer of a very intense philosophy. I was particularly reading his *The Will to Power*, and just reading it made me feel more powerful. He wrote so much in that book about building a strong will, and about accomplishment through determination and will power. Reading him was great for psyching me up to train and compete.

Similarly, when I was in training for the 1980 Mr. Olympia, to get really psyched Ray and I would quote aloud from G. Gordon Liddy's book, *Will*. At times we would even

"The gym became an arena where I had the opportunity to be a hero."—Mike Mentzer

Mike Mentzer *(left)* declares war on his biceps as brother Ray *(right)* looks on.

refer to the competition itself as a battle and the competitors as our adversaries. We'd arouse our dormant warrior instincts by listening to stirring classical music or hard, driving rock. Each of us had our own pieces of literature or philosophy we'd read, and often—the point is we would deliberately cultivate this attitude to the extreme, using whatever form of mental gymnastics was required, to ensure that our workouts would be as intense as possible. By the time we'd leave for Gold's Gym to work out I could feel in myself an anticipatory anxiety akin to that of a soldier about to engage the enemy.

Upon contact with my "enemy," the weights, my nervous tension would explode in a burst of energy so intense that often the other bodybuilders around us would stop training and watch. We would further incite each other to even more intense efforts with such exhortations as "Rip it out of the wall!" "Throw it through the ceiling!" and "Blitz those lats to hell!" There were instances in which, while waiting to do my next set, I'd be shaking with rage. In addition to being a fun and perhaps even therapeutic way of training, these workouts were, of course, intended to make the greatest possible progress. To say that our aggressive approach was successful would be an understatement. During less than a month—from July 25, 1980, to August 18, 1980—my bodyweight went from 207 to 214 pounds, while tests showed that I had lost three pounds of fat at the same time. My actual lean body mass or muscle gain was 10 pounds, while Ray's was slightly less at 8 pounds. Such spectacular gains in so short a period are to be attributed as much to an inspired, aggressive training attitude as they are to my high-intensity training methodology.

If a beginner could sustain such an attitude and approach to his training indefinitely, he could reach the upper limits of his physical potential in one year. Most bodybuilders find it difficult to ever motivate themselves sufficiently to train as hard as is required to attain their maximum progress. There will be others, however, who can dig deep and find the drive to train harder than they had ever before dreamed possible, to "exceed themselves," as Nietzsche exhorted us to do with his image of the *Ubermensch*, or Overman. These are the individuals who will become tomorrow's champions.

So keep in mind that even the most productive of the high-intensity training principles will prove fruitless if they are approached with a defeatist attitude. Undreamed-of results are just the next workout away if only you'll do as Ray and I did and develop a more aggressive attitude toward your training.

Dig deep and find the drive to train harder than you ever have before . . . exceed yourself!

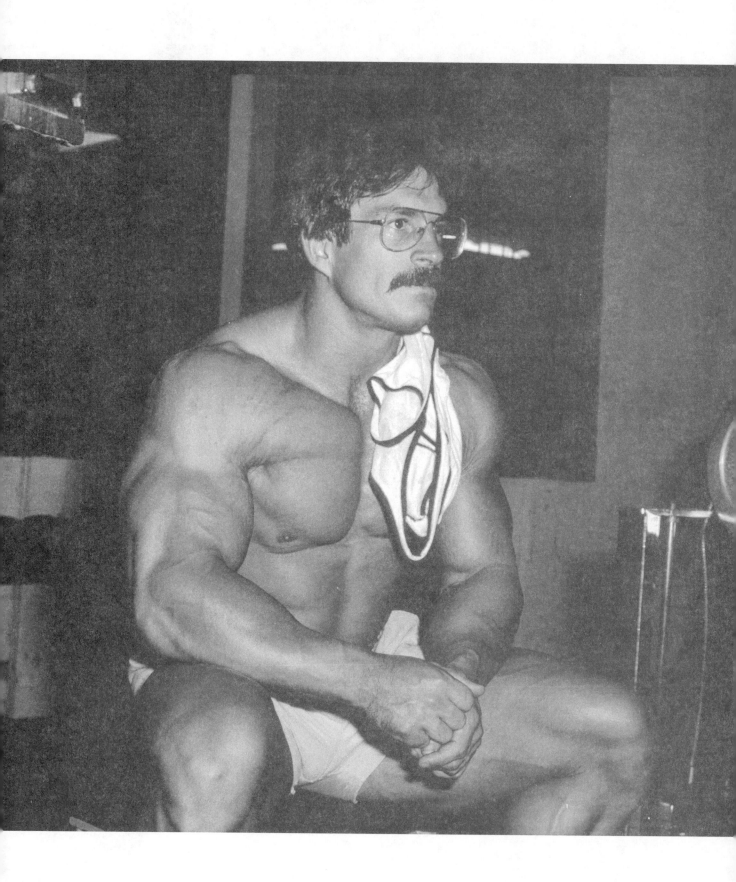

Chapter 20

THE PSYCHOLOGY OF A COMPETITIVE BODYBUILDER

O the puzzle, the thrice tied knot, the deep and
Dark pool, all untied and illumined!
O to speed where there is space enough
and air enough at last!

To have the gag removed from one's mouth!
To have the feeling today or any day I am
    sufficient as I am!

To ascend to leap to the heavens of the love
Indicated in me!
To rise thither with my inebriate soul!

—Walt Whitman, *One Hour to Madness and Joy*

Winning the Mr. Universe in November 1978
bolstered my belief that I was capable of
accomplishing anything I set my mind to. With
the "Big U" firmly in my hip pocket, I set my
sights squarely on the 1979 Mr. Olympia contest to be held in October of that year.

    Now, however, my confidence and motiva-
tion took a quantum leap. Having always envi-
sioned a stellar ascent through the competitive
ranks right from the start, I planned to capture

the most highly coveted professional title—the
Mr. Olympia—in less than three attempts. If it
took more time than that, I cogitated, I would
drop out of competition altogether. I simply
had to ensnare it in a spectacular fashion —or
forget it, I wasn't interested. I did not want to
be known as a dogged veteran who hung in
there until he "earned" it.

    Losing the Mr. Universe a couple times had
actually proved to be a boon because it provided me with the added time necessary to
analyze my competitive preparations in order
to fully grasp the dynamics of proper peaking.
Additional valuable competitive experience was
gained in the early part of 1979 with the bodybuilder's Grand Prix circuit. The first contest,
the Southern Professional Cup, was held in
early February of that year in Miami. My Mr.
Universe victory in Acapulco along with the
attendant benefits—namely poster and book
deals and numerous national television appearances—buoyed my spirits even more; at that
juncture I was literally ready to tackle giants.

    Taking only a brief respite from training
and dieting following my victory in Acapulco, I

Mentzer was able to view certain of his losses in bodybuilding contests as educational opportunities that allowed him to refine his nutritional and training approaches for future contests.

To be at your best on stage requires both a strong body and a strong mind.

resumed serious preparations some six weeks prior to the Miami event, training with the rest-pause principle almost exclusively for the first time, while dieting on a low-calorie/high carbohydrate diet. Maintaining a relatively low bodyfat level after Acapulco, I further honed my musculature, while adding a couple of pounds more muscle. More importantly, the experience provided me with the opportunity to learn better control over the fine-tuning process—how to control subcutaneous water over the last few days of the peaking process just before competition. And I won the Grand Prix in Miami.

Whereas my victory in November of 1978 was marred by a post-contest depression, my second perfect-score-in-a-row victory in Miami left me feeling jubilant afterwards.

Moreover, defeating bodybuilding legend Robby Robinson in the process added to my confidence to such a degree that my certitude that I could win the Mr. Olympia on my first attempt was intransigent.

I should have known that it was not the wont of fate to heap so much good fortune on one individual for so long. In the second of the Grand Prix contests held in Pittsburgh two months later, I garnered yet another perfect score of 300 points, only to lose the overall contest to Robinson in the evening posedown. Robby deserved the triumph as I was less defined in the evening than during the afternoon prejudging due to indiscriminately partaking of various forms of high carbohydrate foods following the prejudging. My perception of myself compared to the rest of the competition, including the Great Robby, during the different stages of the prejudging process and backstage, had so emboldened me that I figured nothing short of a steamroller would keep me from victory. My gluttony, however, made me retain water, smearing what had been my crystal-clear definition earlier in the day. As the evening wore on, I hoped the gradual lessening of my definition was either an illusion or a problem with the lighting. The stark reality was that my ravenous consumption of all and sundry carbohydrates—including pancakes, syrup, fruit, oatmeal, and pastries—had brought a cloud cover over my see-through lining.

Undaunted, I left Pittsburgh for Los Angeles ready to resume my preparation efforts for the third and final leg of the Grand Prix, the Night of the Champions, to be held one month later in New York. The cumulative pressure of training for four shows so close together along with my outside activities and learning of the terminal illness of my mother skyrocketed the stress I was under. I competed in New York but without my erstwhile zest. Neither my body nor my mind was into it. I was like an automaton, going through the motions during the prejudging and feeling like a spectator at the evening's proceedings, watching a frighteningly awesome Robby Robinson trample Danny Padilla into submission. I was more than happy with my third place, feeling lucky to escape alive.

My escape took me to Germany, where, through most of May, German bodybuilding entrepreneur Albert Busek force-fed me Movenpik ice cream during an extensive seminar tour. I must say that Busek's ice cream therapy did help blunt the edge of my defeat. Upon my return to the States at the end of May 1979, I had just enough time to see my mother alive for the last time before she died. In fact, her doctor had kept her artificially alive with her heart beating for my sake with injections of very powerful steroid drugs. After I had seen her, the doctor mercifully ceased the injections, and my mother died a few hours later.

Following my mother's death I was plagued for several weeks by a vague anxiety, which at times threatened to overwhelm me. For a time,

life seemed to lose its luster, and I walked through June and much of July like a somnambulist. By the end of July, having forsaken any attention to diet, with little or no real training, I had slipped into the worst condition of my life. With the Mr. Olympia looming but 10 weeks ahead, I found myself floundering aimlessly in a web of neurotic entanglements. Where the earlier part of the year saw me bounding out of bed every day at 5 A.M., eager at the prospect of the day's contest preparations, now I would languish in the sack until noon, hoping reality would somehow go away by virtue of my simply refusing to acknowledge it.

My confidence had waned considerably during this period, apace the deterioration of my physique. As I lay in bed each morning, my mind would wander at the mercy of my subconscious, allowing all manner of defeating self-talk to compound my gnawing uncertainty: "Geez, me in the Mr. Olympia? But that is such hallowed ground, reserved for my heroes, Sergio Oliva, Arnold Schwarzenegger, Larry Scott, et al. What if I don't even place in the top 10? What will my fans think? What will become of my heretofore illustrious career?" Such was the litany that streamed in and out of my dim awareness each morning, much like an irresistible melody one finds oneself repeating over and over. My life in general became problematic, the simplest of tasks taking on a mountainous aspect.

My Gold's forays had become namby-pamby affairs, far from the war with the weights so valiantly waged earlier in the year. More than once, I abruptly terminated a workout before it was over, turned heel, and slunk out the back door. It wasn't until the middle of August, when my brother Ray was finishing his preparations for the Mr. America (and looking otherworldly), that I finally realized time was marching inexorably onward and if I were going to compete at the Mr. Olympia contest in Columbus—and I had to do that!—then I'd better get my ass in gear.

Now that I felt my back was to the wall, the Mr. Olympia contest bore down upon me like a 10-ton boulder. I experienced that "flip of the switch" inside my head that always signaled a

"The value I placed on the Mr. Olympia contest and my winning it had imbued not only my contest preparation with an almost transcendent sense of meaning, it had elevated everything I did—even the most trivial of tasks—to a higher level of existence."—Mike Mentzer

No, in case you're wondering, I didn't have a "secret super-drug." I had, however, discovered a secret of sorts. I'd found that the value I placed on the Mr. Olympia contest and my winning it had imbued not only my contest preparation with an almost transcendent sense of meaning, it had elevated everything I did— even the most trivial of tasks—to a higher level of existence. My *purpose* followed me like a shadow; even taking out the garbage was a joy. Once, when I ran into a female bodybuilding friend of mine on the street, she said she could feel my energy a block away. I felt (to put it somewhat poetically) that I was plugged into the deep-centered rhythm of the cosmos. In fact, I felt all of a piece. Never was I at cross-purposes. I had dropped all guest appearances during my Mr. Olympia preparations, temporarily put aside my writing for the body-building magazines, and invested every iota of energy I could muster in my training.

The last month before the contest, my training partner and I would meet an hour before each workout at the coffee shop down the street from the gym for a couple espressos and a round of muscle summitry. We'd discuss our plans for that day's workout and generally psych each other up. For us the gym became a Wagnerian landscape where we made our bid for immortality. Full of controlled fury, we'd exhort each other to greater and greater and still greater efforts each and every workout. At one point, about a week from countdown, I was taking a five-mile run down the grassy middle of San Vincente Boulevard in Santa Monica when I became acutely aware of the streams of energy careening through my entire being. I had to stifle a belly laugh for fear of appearing maniacal to the other joggers.

When I woke up on the morning of the contest, I found myself in the grip of a peaking experience. Looking in the mirror at the final result of 10 weeks of Herculean effort, I gave in to that belly laugh, realizing that I was in the best condition of my life. I proceeded to the weigh-in and prejudging "adrenalized," anxious to strip down for the coterie of photographers, journalists, and rubbernecks. What a feeling! The biggest contest of my life, and I had hit my peak perfectly, predictably, and

transformation that would radically alter my psyche; not only was I again leaping out of bed in the dark early morning hours, but I found it difficult at times to go to sleep at all the night before, so exciting was the prospect of each new day's challenge. Along with this marvelous change in my psyche was an equally astounding change in my appearance. No longer did my spot checks in the mirrors at Gold's meet a howling silence from the peanut gallery; now they summoned a gaggle of wide-eyed habitues. "Damn, Mentzer," I'd hear, "you didn't look that good last month—or last *week* even." "Boy, are Robby, Zane, and Padilla in for a shock!" "Hey, Mentzer, do you have some secret super-drug or something?"

methodically, with no guesswork. Everyone who had seen me throughout the preceding week predicted a win for me. Bodybuilding magnate Joe Weider and ace physique photographer Russ Warner, who had already photographed both Robby Robinson and Frank Zane (the two heavily tipped as my greatest challenges in the contest), thought I was better, but their judgments were merely icing on the cake. I was in winning condition and I knew it. If only every human being could experience such elation for but a single moment of his or her life. Whew! This was the day I knew I'd never forget.

Although I would win the heavyweight Mr. Olympia division, I ended up losing the overall title to Zane, despite emerging from the pre-judging with another perfect score. Nevertheless, I walked away from the affair with an enormous sense of pride and accomplishment. Of even greater personal significance than having won my class and second place overall in my first Mr. Olympia, was my realization that what I enjoyed most about bodybuilding competition was not the thrill of victory but the *process*, the months of demanding preparations, drawing upon all my personal efficacy, not only physically but intellectually, emotionally, and spiritually.

I learned from this that the actual contests, like the consummation of all goals, are but single points, standing out like glowing peaks against the tapestry of our lives. It's the travel from peak to peak, the interior process of goal fulfillment in which one must seek the enjoyment—that is what makes life worth living.

"When I woke up on the morning of the contest, I found myself in the grip of a peaking experience."
—Mike Mentzer

Chapter 21

BECOMING AN OLYMPIAN

What our human emotions seem to require is the sight of the struggle going on. . . . Sweat and human effort, human nature strained to its uttermost and on the rack, yet getting through alive, then turning its back on its success to pursue another more rare and arduous still—this is the sort of thing the presence of which inspires us.

—William James, *What Makes a Life Significant*

Ever since Joe Weider created the Mr. Olympia contest back in 1965, the competition's significance has percolated throughout the world of bodybuilding. Acutely aware that an insidious dullness was coming over the sport, Weider snatched victory from the jaws of mediocrity with his greatest contribution to bodybuilding.

Among the plethora of physique contests held each year from the Mr. America to the Grand Prix Finals, none excites the crowd like the parade of Olympians. Like the old gods atop that fabled Greek mountain, today's Mr. Olympia contenders breathe a rarefied atmosphere, while lesser mortals watch them play out the archetypal human drama.

To make it as far as the Olympian stage the bodybuilder must have a mind as strong as his body. According to Dr. Charles Garfield, an expert on the psychological aspects of peak performance, the Olympians are driven by a quest for immortality that motivates men far beyond fame and fortune. Dr. Garfield has termed this drive the "Olympian Complex," or that innate striving toward excellence and self-actualization that exists in all of us.

In contrast to Garfield's Olympian Complex, we humans also possess a dark counterpart, the "Jonah Complex," first described by the American psychologist Abraham Maslow. One day Maslow asked his students, "Which of you expects to achieve greatness in his chosen field?" After a long silence, Maslow asked, "If not you, who then?" It was only then that the students began to see his point, with a subtext implying the power of the fallacy of insignificance. If you are subject to that fallacy, you accept as certainty that you are unlucky,

"This everlasting struggle that the powers of light and Eros wage with those of darkness and Thanatos in our psyches provides all of us with the opportunity for valor."—Mike Mentzer

unworthy, or unimportant; in other words, you have been swallowed by the Jonah Complex.

It is the nature of the relationship between the Olympian Complex and the Jonah Complex in each of us that determines our success and our failure. Although both premises exist simultaneously in most of us, how much one or the other predominates determines whether we move forward and how far, or whether we stagnate in our own self-underestimation. This everlasting struggle that the powers of light and Eros wage with those of darkness and Thanatos in our psyches provides all of us with the opportunity for valor. In our desire to witness "the spectacle of human nature strained to its uttermost and on the rack," most of us fail to see the potential for heroism within each of us. Heroism need not be looked for in bloody battles or raging fires. It can be found in every gym around the world. It is while struggling against the heaviest weights a human body can move that the demand for courage is incessant. There, somewhere, every day of the year, is human nature truly on the rack.

THE UPPER LIMITS

In the 1960s brain research demonstrated that humans could control delicate internal processes long believed to be impossible to control consciously. In the laboratory, people were trained to speed up and slow down their heartbeat, to alter electrical activity on their skin surface, and even to fire a single motor nerve. Barbara Brown, a pioneer biofeedback researcher, has remarked that this deep biological awareness reflects the mind's ability to alter every physiological system, every cell in the body. As bodybuilders, we naturally ask if such abilities can be used to alter our muscle cells, the appearance of our bodies. The answer is an unqualified *yes!* What evidence can I adduce to prove my point? Boyer Coe is evidence. Frank Zane is evidence, Arnold Schwarzenegger, Larry Scott, Lee Haney, Dorian Yates—any of the Olympians—are evidence of the powers of mind. Arnold Schwarzenegger is no soothsayer. When he started training, he didn't know what his future had in store for him. Neither did I

"It is while struggling against the heaviest weights a human body can move that the demand for courage is incessant."—Mike Mentzer

"It is virtually impossible for the average man or woman to understand the extraordinary effort involved in building an Olympian physique."—Mike Mentzer

when I began as a skinny 12-year-old from Pennsylvania with plenty of desire and nothing else.

Now this is not to downplay the importance of genetics in determining upper limits. But potential is only the expression of a possibility, something that can be assessed accurately only in retrospect. In other words, you'll never know how good you might become unless you try. And that quite simply is the answer to the question: who are the Olympians? The Olympians have made on a deep spiritual level a passionate commitment to reach the upper limits of their physical potential. While many of us may consider the quest for fame and fortune the chief motivation of the advanced bodybuilder, that is a very small part. The rest goes much, much deeper. It is virtually impossible for the average man or woman to understand the extraordinary effort involved in building an Olympian physique.

Actualizing the Olympian Complex requires that we tap the enormous powers of the unconscious. A formula for gaining access to these powers and achieving Olympian greatness is to combine goal-directed passion with physiologic uniqueness and proper training. Where does the drive for excellence, the Olympian Complex, derive from? Consider the case of Al Oerter, four-time Olympic gold

medal–winner in the discus, who chose to train on a small high school field with no coaches and no training partners, under conditions much more modest than his stature would warrant. When asked how he could train so hard under such conditions, Oerter replied, "I'm not competing with other discus throwers; I'm competing with history."

It is through establishing goals of greatness that you let loose the powerful hidden reserves of the unconscious for the kind of performance that leads to Olympian accomplishment. The sustained motivation to reach the top in any arena is internal, and this motivation can be consciously cultivated in everyone to help reach the upper limits of human potential. This suggests that champions are not born, but made.

Scientists in the former USSR have developed an entire field of study called *anthropomaximology*, which is the study of the upper limits of human capabilities. By researching those individuals who have reached the pinnacle in their chosen area of endeavor, the Soviets have been able to map out precisely what is required to become a peak performer, an Olympian. Scientists in the United States are also becoming more interested in this type of research and are learning how to increase motivation and achievement to superhuman strata.

An Olympian knows that a limit is merely a temporary level of accomplishment that can be surpassed.

THESE ARE THE OLYMPIANS

By taking a look at some of the specific characteristics of those who have achieved the highest levels in bodybuilding, we might better understand what is required to actually reach the Olympian level. Here is a profile of an Olympian bodybuilder:

An Olympian Transcends Limits

First, he is very good at transcending personal and cultural limits. He knows that a limit is merely a temporary level of accomplishment that can be surpassed. Never satisfied with continuing to exist and operate within his existing limits, the Olympian is always struggling to do one more rep, to build just a little more mass here or there, to get even more ripped. He has developed the capacity to inject a high degree of cultivated purpose into his workouts and contest preparations.

An Olympian Focuses on the Positive

Second, the Olympian has learned to focus on the positive. Rather than dwelling upon his mistakes, defeats, and physical shortcomings as negatives, he views them as inevitable challenges that provide valuable opportunities for learning and self-correction on the road to success. Many bodybuilders focus so much on a physical shortcoming that their "will batteries" run dry and they become paralyzed by inertia. An Olympian like Boyer Coe, on the other hand, suffering from a deficiency in the abdominal region, perfected the rest of his physique so that the deficiency would be less noticeable. While some will view a defeat as a personal failure and stop trying, an Olympian analyzes what caused his defeat and uses the information to do better in his next contest. I recall talking to Valerie Coe (Boyer's wife at the time), the morning after the Sydney Mr. Olympia in 1980. She said that as she and Boyer were getting ready to go to sleep, all Boyer could do was rehash his performance. On and on he went until finally, before he fell asleep, he muttered, "Valerie, I know I can do it next year!" As Boyer Coe's attitude suggests,

Olympians are progressionists—not perfectionists.

Olympians are not perfectionists but progressionists.

This ability to direct their thoughts and attitude to the positive is not innate. It is something the Olympians have trained themselves to do. Top champs have actually taught themselves to direct their attitude towards success. They have learned to monitor their thoughts and attitude, and when they see a negative thought pattern developing, they nip it in the bud by willfully generating a positive one. Research has shown that a negative thought attracts similar thoughts. The corollary of this is that so does a positive thought attract positive thoughts. Neurons carrying positive thoughts have the power to involve more and more neurons in their habitual activity. If these positive thoughts are continued, a chain reaction begins that can become invaluable as a tool for transforming one's physique.

An Olympian Sets Goals

Third, Olympians are masters of goal setting. Man is a future-oriented animal. He gets the best from himself only when he has something to look forward to. In order to develop the mental preparedness required to train with ever-increasing Olympian intensity, the bodybuilder must have goals.

• *Short-Range Goals:* An Olympian sees each workout as an obstacle to be surmounted. Many keep accurate records of each workout as a means of measuring intensity increases more precisely. I always made it a daily practice of sitting down before each workout and reviewing the poundages, sets, and reps I employed in the previous workout. Then I would write down my goals for the upcoming workout.

• *Long-Range Goals:* The Olympian has learned that without knowing where it is he wants to go, he'll never get anywhere. His goal of winning the Mr. Olympia is a powerful stimulant that increases the meaning of his workouts. Meaning stimulates willpower and vitality, which, in turn, provide the Olympian with increased access to the hidden reserves that make superhuman workouts his daily fare. For those whose cups runneth over with desire and meaning, there will be no limits to their accomplishments. Nothing short of the Mr. Olympia title will satiate their appetites to achieve.

Mike Mentzer always made the point in his standing-room-only seminars that "in order to develop the mental preparedness required to train with ever-increasing Olympian intensity, the bodybuilder must have both short- and long-range goals."

An Olympian Embraces Success

Fourth, Olympians have learned to overcome their fear of success and the unknown. Success is highly alluring, yet when a bodybuilder approaches the Olympian level he is confronted with increased responsibilities and pressures to compete. If he has not yet learned how to cope consciously with these anxiety-producing demands, he devises unconscious methods to sabotage himself only inches away from pay dirt. The bodybuilder's journey to Olympian heights can be viewed as taking place on a pyramid. In the beginning the individual bodybuilder finds himself at the base, mixed in the pack of tens of thousands of athletes whose sights are set at the top of the pyramid. If he perseveres, finding bits of success along the way, he will continue to move closer to the top. As the path narrows, however, his chances to continue ascending are reduced. The competition becomes increasingly cutthroat and the bodybuilder who is not prepared psychologically to take the slings and arrows will stop in his tracks or fall back.

As he gets closer to the pyramid's peak, more and more eyes focus on him, making him feel like a stickpin-impaled butterfly being observed under a powerful magnifying glass. And as he continues to win contests, people place greater demands on him at each performance. If he becomes other-directed, that is, if he allows others' expectations to motivate him, the pressure becomes unbearable, as his self-esteem comes to rest more and more on winning. Losing results in disapproval from others and lowered self-esteem for the bodybuilder, which will prevent him from pressing upward toward the peak.

The bodybuilder at the peak of the pyramid, a Mr. Olympia, does not fear success or failure because he has learned to be a self-motivator. He has developed the liberating knack to compete with himself, or with something abstract like history. For the Olympian, success no longer depends on winning and losing, nor on the extrinsic rewards that come from winning contests (fame, trophies, money). To buttress his self-esteem, the Olympian becomes a self-actualizer, one who looks increasingly to intrinsic rewards for his motivation. His desire to gain inner mastery—by proving his excellence and competence to himself—makes him immune to the routine anxieties and pressures that often attend success.

An Olympian Utilizes Mental Visualization

Fifth, the Olympian is experienced at practicing imagery and rehearsing mentally. In his book *Psycho-Cybernetics,* Maxwell Maltz explains why this approach is crucial to success. He states: "Clinical psychologists have proven beyond a shadow of a doubt that the human nervous system cannot tell the difference between an actual experience and an experience imagined vividly and in detail."

The greatest Olympian of all, Arnold Schwarzenegger, has applied this intuitively for

"The bodybuilder at the peak of the pyramid, a Mr. Olympia, does not fear success or failure because he has learned to be a self-motivator."—Mike Mentzer

"The Olympian becomes a self-actualizer, one who looks increasingly to intrinsic rewards for his motivation. His desire to gain inner mastery—by proving his excellence and competence to himself—makes him immune to the routine anxieties and pressures that often attend success."—Mike Mentzer

years to enhance his bodybuilding efforts. When training for a contest, Arnold would actually visualize his biceps, for instance, as huge mountains filling the gym. I, too, have relied heavily on mental imagery to enhance my physique. Three weeks of training before my Mr. America win in 1976, I barely slept a wink, yet I would arise each morning refreshed and anxious to get to the gym. All night before each workout I would stare at the ceiling as though it were a movie screen and visualize the following day's workout. I would try to see how successful it would be; I'd picture each rep of each set, so as to overcome progressively heavier weight requirements. Finally, during my last week of nearly sleepless nights I saw myself on my mental movie screen as the winner of the competition. I pictured everything that would

lead up to the moment when I'd be announced as the winner—from my entrance at the Felt Forum to my exuberant acceptance of the winner's trophy.

The imagination is a direct link to the subconscious, and as such is a powerful tool. One cannot actualize his goals until he visualizes them clearly in the mind's eye. The Olympians have an intuitive grasp at least of the potency of such a mental technique. Others have realized that this ability is as important as physical training and have actively cultivated it.

THE FINAL FRONTIER?

Bodybuilders are often so obsessive in their search for new training theories, nutritional

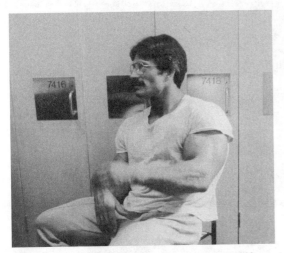

"The human mind is thought to be the only self-evolving thing that exists, and the more evolved, the more we develop its natural capacities, the more control it will give us over our bodies."—Mike Mentzer

"One cannot actualize his goals until he visualizes them clearly in the mind's eye."—Mike Mentzer

information, or new possibilities in drugs and equipment that might provide them with just the edge they need to launch them to the Olympian level, that they tend to neglect the mind and its training as a means of enhancing their physiques. They spend so much time looking outside to new scientific advancements and technology, that they overlook the inner possibilities of the greatest transformative device in the world: the human mind.

The human mind is thought to be the only self-evolving thing that exists, and the more evolved, the more we develop its natural capacities, the more control it will give us over our bodies. It is doubtful that we will see many more innovations in scientific training theories or technological advancements that will provide the bodybuilder with the means of upping the training intensity required to effect a giant leap forward in the existing standard of bodybuilding excellence. Going beyond the limits of intensity that bodybuilders are now achieving requires greater access to the hidden transformative powers that lie for the most part dormant in the unconscious. And we know

now that this can be done only by incorporating mental training with physical training.

John Lilly, psychologist and dolphin researcher, has said, "The only limit man has is that which his mind conceives." Having seen the current crop of Mr. Olympia competitors, it is breathtaking for us to think that somewhere in the world a young bodybuilder has conceived of a physique of an even higher caliber! It is precisely this kind of belief in the miraculous that will determine who will be tomorrow's Olympians.

Mike Mentzer always chose poses that would project the heroic and inspirational, to communicate a message of man at his best.

Chapter 22

THE BEST IS WITHIN YOU

I presume from the fact that you are reading this book that you are a hardcore bodybuilder, that your interest in bodybuilding has transcended the level of the casual trainee, and you'd like to be a physique champion, a superstar.

"Ah, yes, Mr. Mentzer," I can almost hear your mental wheels spinning, "I think about being a champion every day, but it's turning out to be a more difficult task than I'd imagined. Now I'm beginning to have my doubts. Geez, maybe I'll never make it."

By way of solace, I'll have you know that all of us, including the top champs, have fallen prey to the ogre of self-doubt on occasion. The fact that a stray bubble of doubt percolates through your thoughts from time to time should not be a cause of any undue fretting and nail biting. If, on the other hand, you continue to focus on your fears and doubts, they will rapidly escalate in frequency and dimensions until soon they'll take on the character of a tempest in a teapot.

How does one prevent one's fears from becoming a ball and chain of self-doubt where one's wings of confidence should have grown? I can guarantee you that any degree of wishing, hoping, or praying will not eliminate your fears, doubts, or sense of inadequacy. The only way is through the understanding of the first principle elucidated in this book: the principle of identity, which reveals that your biologically distinguishable trait as a human being is your rational faculty, your ability to reason. Only through the fullest possible use of this faculty to make a rational, realistic assessment of the facts regarding your situation and possible future, will you keep on the even psychological keel necessary to reach your goals. You might begin by attempting to grasp just how arduous and difficult a task you've chosen; reconsider the material provided in Chapters 1 and 2— just how realistic are your chances of becoming a champion bodybuilder?

This is not stated to dampen your enthusiasm or destroy your motivation. Developing a clear and accurate picture of what is required to become a champion is the first important step toward achieving that goal. Realizing the immensity of the task you've undertaken will make you aware of the need for a long-term commitment to hard training and proper dieting. Picture your goal of becoming a great bodybuilder as a long journey. Like all long journeys, yours begins with a small step; actually it's made up of innumerable such small

Developing a clear and accurate picture of what is required to become a champion is the first important step toward achieving that goal.

steps, which will, of course, lead to your destination.

Even if becoming a top title winner is your ultimate long-range goal, you will find it easier to sustain motivation and a positive attitude by creating and realizing the short-term goals that you know are within reach. Formulating far-fetched, unrealistic goals only sets up a pattern of failure and hence frustration, dampening motivations. Don't set a goal of gaining 10 pounds of muscle each week or month when you've heard it over and over from all authorities that a 10-pound gain of muscle per year is more realistic. Don't get discouraged if you don't see weight gains on the scale every day. If you do, you are getting fat, which is not what your aim is. Don't use the scale as your sole indicator of progress—use strength gains. Are you getting stronger? To get bigger, you must get stronger; and as strength increases usually precede increases in muscle mass, use strength as a guide to your progress from high-intensity training.

Set short-term goals. If you can currently squat 225 pounds for 8 reps, aim to squat 250 pounds for 8 reps within four weeks. That's a realistic short-term goal. Remember, ultimate success is built on a series of small successes. Be realistic. Be patient. And now that you possess a more realistic long-term perspective of your bodybuilding career, how do you get the most out of each and every workout? How can you make optimal progress? The answer to these questions is—apart from training in a high-intensity fashion—through your mental attitude.

The greatest resistance encountered on the road to athletic achievement is not the body, but the mind. It's not the weights, the equipment, the weather, or astrology; it's your own mind. A well-trained body is capable of near-maximum or maximum effort at any time. But the kind of effort it takes to build a great physique imposes demands of a high order on the body, which is why such training is so productive. But the mind, in an effort to protect the precious, limited reserves of resources that are used up in maximum efforts, will throw up all kinds of roadblocks. "I'd better not push too hard, I might hurt myself," or, "Why should I push so hard when the other guys in the gym don't push half as hard as I do anyway?"

This kind of mental jabberwocky that often precedes a hard workout is the result of a general mental and physical disinclination to go all out in your training so as to preserve and conserve energy and resources. To be stimulated to break through such mental barriers, and to perform at consistently higher levels, some unusual stimulus must fill you with emotional excitement or some idea of necessity must induce you to make the extra effort of will. You must enter each training session excited by some idea of necessity. Well, that shouldn't be so hard. You want to be the best you can be, don't you? If that doesn't get you excited, nothing will. As I related elsewhere in this book, the last three weeks before I won the Mr. America contest, I barely slept at all, that's how excited I was. Despite little sleep, I was never tired. I would lie awake staring at the ceiling as though it were a movie screen, visualizing in detail the next day's workout. I would see myself using heavier weights as though they were lighter, and I would picture myself pushing harder than my previous workout. During that last week of sleepless nights, I would see myself on my mental movie screen as the win-

"A well-trained body is capable of near-maximum or maximum effort at any time." Mentzer exerts himself maximally on a set of Universal machine shrugs.

"To be stimulated to break through mental barriers, and to perform at consistently higher levels, some unusual stimulus must fill you with emotional excitement or some idea of necessity must induce you to make the extra effort of will."—Mike Mentzer

"Making a passionate commitment to succeed and creatively visualizing your workout beforehand will help enormously."—Mike Mentzer

ner of the contest. And you know something? I made more progress during those last three weeks than I'd made during the previous nine months.

If you go into the gym having given your workout no forethought, it will invariably end up a namby-pamby affair resulting in little or no progress. You've literally got to approach each workout like a savage warrior, full of rage and fury! Before each workout sit down quietly somewhere by yourself and focus on your goal and the value you hope to gain by achieving it. If you are fully convinced that being a top bodybuilder is what you really want, then focusing on your goal will liberate a tremendous energy to meet the task ahead.

Man cannot live constantly on the heartbeat of the moment as animals do. Man's long-term survival hinges on his willingness to use his long-range vision. This, however, requires an act of choice. To think, conceptualize, or look long-range requires a choice on your part. You must ask yourself, "Do I really want to be a champ? What is required to do so?" Making a passionate commitment to succeed and creatively visualizing your workout beforehand will help enormously.

Reading about the great accomplishments of others may fill you with excitement for your own training. In the past, and even now on occasion, if I need a little motivational boost, I'll read a novel by my favorite writer/philosopher, Ayn Rand. Rand's novels project the very explicit notion that man's proper stature is not one of mediocrity, failure, frustration, or defeat, but one of achievement, strength, and nobility. In short, man can and ought to be a hero. Don't fall into the trap of believing that successful people possess some mysterious gift, some mystical endowment, and then tear your hair out wondering if you've been so blessed. If you're waiting for some automatic inspiration to put a fire under you, well forget it. If you truly desire to make maximum progress, then it's up to you and you alone to cultivate that germ of ambition that lies within.

The enormous energy that fueled the success of all the great bodybuilding champions can be yours. It's not as though some were born with it and not others. And you can't get it from a pill. All of us possess a will, a certain amount of drive from deep within that motivates us to act. Our ability to summon this drive is dependent on the meaning and value we place on certain activities, like bodybuilding. If your desire is strong enough, your willpower and sense of meaning will act like two mirrors enhancing your strength and vitality.

Renunciation is not part of my vocabulary, and you should exclude it from yours. Don't vanish into the vast swamp of mediocrity by believing that maturity is gained by abandoning one's ideals, values, goals, and ultimately self-esteem. Hold on to that noble vision. Don't betray that fire. Give it shape, reality, and purpose. Let your muscles serve as an expression of your victorious will and your glorious reason. Don't just be a bodybuilder—be the greatest bodybuilder that you can possibly be.

"Man's proper stature is not one of mediocrity, failure, frustration, or defeat, but one of achievement, strength, and nobility. In short, man can and ought to be a hero."—Mike Mentzer

Mike Mentzer on stage at the 1980 Mr. Olympia contest—a contest that many journalists, bodybuilders, and fans believe he should have won.

APPENDIX
THE COMPETITIVE BODYBUILDING RECORD OF MIKE MENTZER

1. 1970 Mr. Pennsylvania—AAU, 1st (Age 19)
2. 1971 Mr. America—AAU, 10th
3. 1971 Teen Mr. America—AAU, 2nd
4. 1975 Mr. America—IFBB, Medium, 3rd
5. 1975 Mr. USA—ABBA, Medium, 2nd
6. 1976 Mr. America—IFBB, Overall Winner
7. 1976 Mr. America—IFBB, Medium, 1st
8. 1976 Mr. Universe—IFBB, Middleweight, 2nd
9. 1977 North American Championships—IFBB, Overall Winner
10. 1977 North American Championships—IFBB, Middleweight, 1st
11. 1977 Mr. Universe—IFBB, Heavyweight, 2nd
12. 1978 Mr. Universe—USA vs. the World—IFBB, Heavyweight, 1st (perfect score of 300)
13. 1979 Canada Pro Cup—IFBB, 2nd
14. 1979 Florida Pro Invitational—IFBB, 1st
15. 1979 Night of Champions—IFBB, 3rd
16. 1979 Mr. Olympia—IFBB, Heavyweight, 1st (perfect score of 300)
17. 1979 Pittsburgh Pro Invitational—IFBB, 2nd
18. 1979 Southern Pro Cup—IFBB, 1st
19. 1980 Mr. Olympia—IFBB, 5th
20. 1980 Canada Cup—IFBB, 2nd

Total Contests Entered: 20
Total Contests Won (First Place Finishes): 9
Total Second Place Finishes: 7
Total Third Place Finishes: 2
Total Fifth Place Finishes: 1
Total Tenth Place Finishes: 1

INDEX

ABOUT THE AUTHORS

Mike Mentzer (1951–2001) is the only body-builder ever to win the Mr. Universe competition with a perfect score and the man who pioneered and popularized the notion of high-intensity training. He conducted seminars all over the world and was a columnist for *Iron-man* magazine and former editor-in-chief of *Muscle and Fitness* magazine. He is the author of several bestselling books (*Heavy Duty, The Mentzer Method*) and is considered one of the greatest bodybuilders in history. To learn more about the teachings of Mike Mentzer, you are encouraged to visit the official Mike Mentzer website, mikementzer.com.

John Little is the author of more than 25 books on bodybuilding, martial arts, history, and philosophy, including *Power Factor Training* and *Static Contraction Training* (with Pete Sisco). He is the innovator of the Max Contraction method of bodybuilding/strength training (maxcontraction.com) and was a close friend of Mentzer's for more than two decades. Little's books have sold in excess of 600,000 copies and are published in several languages. Little is also an award-winning documentary filmmaker and his articles have been published in every major health and fitness publication in North America.